Three Steps Forward

Three Steps Forward

VERA DEAN

FABER AND FABER

24 Russell Square

London

First published in mcmlvii
by Faber and Faber Limited
24 Russell Square London W.C.1
Printed in Great Britain by
Latimer Trend & Co Ltd Plymouth
All rights reserved

To my family, Mrs. Collis and her team

May the Lord grant me the strength to accept with serenity the things that cannot be changed.

May He give me the courage to change the things that can and should be changed.

And may He grant me the wisdom to distinguish one from the other.

Contents

1. CHILDHOOD   *page* 9
2. OUT INTO THE WORLD   17
3. A NEW LIFE BEGINS   28
4. SETBACKS AND TEARS   38
5. I LEARN TO TALK   46
6. BRENTWOOD   58
7. SCHOOL   71
8. I BECOME A PERSON   84
9. THE FIRST STEP   97
10. MY TRICYCLE   109
11. THE DARK DAYS   120
12. HOME   131
13. CAMPING WITH THE HANDICAPPED   147
14. HOLIDAY IN FRANCE   165
15. NEW HORIZONS   178
16. THE END AND THE BEGINNING   187

7

I

Childhood

On 26th January 1928, London was in the grip of an icy spell. Those few brave people who dared to set foot outside their homes had to wear sackcloth on their feet to prevent them slipping on the treacherous roads. Even so, several people in a little back-street in Kennington fell on the glassy pavements and were taken to hospital with broken arms and legs.

In a two-roomed basement flat in this same little back-street quite a lot of activity was taking place. A small family was preparing for another blessed event, although it would hardly be true to say that it had been looked forward to as blessed. Father worked on London's Underground Railway and with a seven-year-old son and four-year-old daughter already to care for there was neither money nor space to spare for a third child. Nevertheless, as the time approached, Mother made the necessary preparations to welcome the new-born babe into the world, and then, suddenly, I was born.

My entrance was quite unceremonious. Mother was so unaware of my impending approach that she merely got out of bed and dropped me on the mat. I was promptly named 'Vera Mat-ilda'!

The small flat was immediately thrown into a state of turmoil. Father dashed out to get the midwife, who was unfortunately out on an emergency call, and panic-stricken he combed the neighbourhood for a substitute. After a short while, which to Mother seemed like eternity, Father and a nurse arrived to find me still attached to mother by the umbilical cord, which, by this time was twisted tightly round my neck. Nurse announced, 'She is asphyxiated' and began to revive me by touching my lips with brandy and plunging my body into alternate bowls of hot and cold water.

After several hours her perseverance was rewarded and I began to show signs of life, but nurse obligingly told Mother, 'This child will never be any use—she'll never be like a normal child!' Mother, grief-stricken, despairingly asked whether in that case it would not be better to let that small spark of life flicker out, but the horrified nurse replied that it was her duty to keep the child alive.

After a day and night of continual attention, during which time every second appeared to be my last, I was transferred to hospital where I stayed for a fortnight and was then discharged as a normal baby. I gained weight but made very little other progress, and the only sound that passed my lips was a continuous moan, rather like the squealing of a young pig. It was impossible to keep food down as I vomited continually; my small body was alternately stiff and limp, but by some miracle I survived and grew.

Soon it became apparent that the midwife's dreadful prophecy was coming true. At the age of two I did not sit up and made no attempt to cry or feed myself. My clothes were always wet from incessant dribbling—a habit which was not checked until I was fifteen.

The Welfare Clinic said there was nothing wrong, I was merely backward. This opinion was confirmed by the numerous doctors Mother consulted. Eventually, at the age of two and a half years, it was diagnosed that I had cerebral palsy (or spastic paralysis as it was then called) and I was admitted to a Children's Hospital where I stayed for three years.

I was put into the ward for 'spastics' and spent most of the time in bed because I was so handicapped. It was still impossible to sit up without help (owing to my great unsteadiness in all movement). To overcome this the nurses would prop me up with pillows and I would tighten every muscle in an effort to stay rigidly in that position. My body would become very tense and my neck seemed to disappear as my head became hunched between my shoulders. My arms curled right up and my toes and legs turned inwards. I was at that time, and remained for many years, like a little wriggling ball.

At the age of four I became very ill with peritonitis and once again life hung in the balance. For a fortnight Mother and Father stayed in the hospital and were told by the doctors that they should not grieve for me as it was a hopeless case and they marvelled at my will to live. But after much tender nursing, and to the complete amazement of the doctors, I recovered.

Shortly after this the doctors decided that there was nothing further they could do for me and I was discharged.

At that time we were living in a second-floor flat at Streatham. We lived there until I was seven years old and weighed about four stone, and Mother realized that soon it would be impossible for her to carry me and the wheel-chair up and down the stairs. My only means of getting about indoors was by a peculiar kind of jumping forward on my knees—rather like the hopping of a frog—and as I wore boots all the time, the continual thud, thud on the ceiling of the flat below caused considerable annoyance to our neighbours. Unwittingly, I was the cause of many arguments because Mother refused to keep me strapped into a chair all day, and directly I started crawling about the lady downstairs retaliated by knocking on her ceiling with a broomstick. She really couldn't be blamed, poor woman, the noise must have been awful, and our only solution was to move to a house. Luckily the present-day housing shortage didn't exist then and it wasn't long before we found a small house at Brixton, where we spent seven happy years.

The house was rather small, but it had a fairly long back garden and here I would sit in the toy car that Mother had bought from a woman whose cerebral palsied son had outgrown it. I used to go up and down the path, not using the pedals, that was far too slow, but by pushing on the ground with my feet in a sort of walking movement. I played for hours in that car and the handle would get hot where I grabbed it so tightly. Years later the car, which was made of aluminium, was given as scrap metal to help the war effort and I felt as though I had lost a friend.

It was still impossible for me to sit upright on a chair or on the floor without support but my parents were determined that I should walk so they bought me a baby's pram for a toy. Every Sunday morning, after church, my sister Gladys would put her big doll in one end of it, sit me in the other, and take me out for a walk. How I wished that that doll was mine; it was made of china and had real brown hair. When we came to a quiet street, Gladys would take me out of the pram and make me push it. I was so proud of that pram and it was a thrill to push it.

Another toy I had was a second-hand tricycle that had been specially built for a cerebral palsied boy. It was larger than a normal child's tricycle and I could not use it until Father had made a wooden box seat with a strap to go round my waist, so that I could not fall off. The next step was to keep my feet from flying off the pedals, this was done by putting leather straps over my toes. I loved going up to the Common on that bike, as once I got there I was allowed to go where I liked. Steering was not easy, but that did not matter as I could go across the grass, in and out of the big trees and round and round again. It was great fun. That bike was like a magic carpet—it took me into another world where for a while I was free from the family and quite independent. To go where I liked was heaven, I felt like a bird let out of a cage and was always sorry when it was time to go home.

But most of my time was spent either on the floor in the living-room or on a mat in the garden. Dad made a swing for Gladys and my brother Stanley and on sunny days I would kneel on the grass and watch them swinging backward and forward, up and down for the sheer joy of being alive. I longed to do the same but could not sit on the swing alone, so Father made me a very big baby swing that I could not fall out of. The hours I spent on that swing! I could push on the ground with my feet and when I got high I could see into the next garden where the children were running and playing. When the children saw me they would stop and stare, and unaccountably frightened, I would call for Mummy to take me indoors.

Two incidents that occurred at about that time stand out in my mind. The first happened on a Saturday afternoon when everyone went out leaving Stanley to look after me. A favourite game of Stan's was to get all my rag and rubber dolls and throw them up and down the passage that ran through the house. He was not very kind to my dolls and they used to fly everywhere, but I loved it. When we had been playing for a long time Stanley decided to go and buy some sweets, so he said, 'Wait here a minute, Vera, while I go out and get some dolly mixtures (the only sweets that I could eat). You'll be all right.'

'Yes,' I replied, and off he went. For the first time in my life I was really alone and I was very frightened. I started to cry, then the cry became a scream; I screamed and screamed; I was frightened that ghosts would come and take me away and I was rigid with fear. Stanley was gone for about ten minutes, but it seemed a day. When he returned and asked me why I was crying, I lied and said that I wanted to go to the W.C., as he would not have believed the truth.

The second incident happened when Stanley left school at fifteen and went to work for the B.B.C. He was very keen to make progress and thought a good way to learn would be by getting old radio sets and pulling them apart to see how they worked. One day he put one of these sets in the large cupboard under the stairs and took a wire from it into the sitting-room where he attached it to a microphone. Then he told me to wait until Dad came in and just talk. Stanley sat in a chair with a book and when Father came in I said, 'Daddy, do you know where I am? I do love you, Daddy.'

Poor man, he looked everywhere for me and when he gave

up Stanley told him what he had done. Father picked me up from the floor and amidst our laughter he said how glad he was that nothing had happened to me.

I have always loved drawing and painting and many happy hours were spent kneeling on the floor, holding the pencil with one hand on top of the other, and dribbling profusely while trying to produce something which looked like a picture. My favourite subject was Father. He was a handsome man, but he had some cysts on the top of his head so, of course, I was always drawing him with lots of bumps. To other people it didn't matter very much what I drew as all my pictures looked like scribble.

Another favourite pastime was playing with my dolls. There were about twenty of them; big ones, small ones, china and celluloid ones, teddy bears and dogs; each one was known by name. The game I always played was 'hospitals'. I did not know much about school and very little happened at home, but I did know all about hospitals. How many times I made my dolls walk up and down or try to feed themselves! But my dolls did not get any better because I did not improve, and when I was tired of playing with them I would dream of the day when I could help other people. My wildest and most satisfying dream was to be a doctor and help other people handicapped like myself.

I knew how to give my dolls treatment because every week Mother and I were taken by ambulance to the hospital where I was given massage and remedial exercises. This pattern was followed for several years going from one hospital to another, but sooner or later each doctor gave the same verdict, 'We're sorry, Mother, but we can't do any more for your child.'

Because of my speech difficulty I could not talk much, so I used to tell myself stories. At the same time I heard a lot of very frightening plays on the radio and they seemed so real that they became part of my life. I believed in fairies, witches and ghosts, but did not tell anyone as I thought they would think me silly and send me away for ever.

Although I was now eight years of age I could make no more than a few noises with my throat. Somehow the family usually knew what I was trying to say, but to outsiders I was dumb, so it was decided that I should attend hospital for speech therapy. The therapist was a very kind person and as she did not think that one lesson a week was sufficient she used to come home to help me. She had received her training from the speech therapist to King George VI and with tremendous patience she taught me to talk, though still not very intelligibly. But at least I could ask for what *I* wanted and the family could understand me better.

At about this time Father heard of a place at Clapham Junction where two women were doing very good work by giving sun-ray and electrical treatment to sick and crippled people. So once a week, winter and summer, Mother put me in my wheelchair and pushed me the six or seven miles each way. At the centre I was stripped of all clothes and put on a bed under a big sun-ray lamp. This was followed by electrical treatment with a thing like a hair-dryer. It was lovely and warm and soothing, but the only effect it seemed to have was to turn my skin brown, and since then I have always looked rather sunburnt.

I was now eleven years of age and the Education Authorities thought it was time I had some lessons, so for a period of about six months I was taken by ambulance each day to the local school for physically handicapped children. I looked forward to going, but when I got there my joy turned to disappointment and fear because I was made to sit on a chair at a table to write. Although I was tied to the chair it needed all my concentration to sit upright or I would have fallen off, and to write while sitting at a table was just impossible. I could not be taught to read because of my speech difficulty, and when the teachers, in desperation, gave me toys to play with, my shaky hands simply knocked them to the floor. It was very boring just watching the other children and as I could not control my emotions I cried to be taken home nearly every day. After a while the teachers realized my difficulties and put me in a play-pen on the floor of the classroom. Here I felt much more secure and nobody minded about the mess if I tried to draw or paint. Gradually the people around me became friends instead of strangers and I was less apprehensive of my surroundings, but with the outbreak of war the school was closed and lessons (such as they were) ended.

In July 1939 Dad kept getting a pain in his chest and the doctors diagnosed indigestion. Months passed and he seemed to get no better so we decided to spend a fortnight's holiday at the sea in the hope that the fresh air would do him some good. A week before we were due to go away Dad's leave was suddenly cancelled and on the 3rd September, instead of being on a train to happiness, I was sitting on his lap listening to the awful announcement on the radio that war had been declared. Stunned by this news we sat motionless for a while, but hardly had the Prime Minister finished speaking when the air-raid warning sounded for the first time and Dad jumped to his feet to rush me into the Anderson shelter in the garden. Stanley followed at his heels while Mum stood at the front gate imploring strangers to come in and share our shelter. While this was going on Gladys was sitting in the bath—a large tin one situated in the kitchen. Everyone had to pass through the kitchen to get to the garden and Gladys, covered with confusion, was torn between her natural modesty and her desire to save her skin. Within minutes she, too, was in the shelter, wrapped in no more than a bath towel. Her first remark was, 'I wouldn't have minded so much but I have only just got into the bath and haven't had time to wash myself yet!'

By Christmas of that year Dad was very ill and when he came home from work on Christmas Day he leaned on the table trying to get his breath and in great pain. On Boxing Day he got up and tried to go to work again but Mum insisted that he should go to hospital instead; and on the 20th January 1940, he died of a tumour on the lung. The day after my birthday he was laid to rest.

2

Out into the World

⤜⟨≋≋⟩⤛

It was a lovely summer day in June 1940 when I was taken to Queen Mary's Hospital. The black hospital car was large and comfortable and a nurse accompanied me on the journey. I tried to smile as I waved good-bye to Mother, but it was not easy as I had never been away from her for any length of time except as a baby, and I took a last long look at the house I loved so well. I will always look back on that place as a little heaven. We three children had been so happy there, and now I was starting a new life of my own; a life that I did not want at all, but one that I shall never forget. I felt very sad.

Queen Mary's Hospital is a very big place and is approached by a long drive with trees and shrubs. The sunlight was dancing in and out of the trees, but my world seemed very black and stormy. When I saw this, to me, horrible avenue of trees I knew that we were almost there and, becoming very frightened, I began to cry.

After admission I was examined and sent to the appropriate ward to be bathed and shampooed by two nurses. I tried to tell them that Mother had given me a bath that morning and washed my hair the night before, but they could not understand what I said.

For the following five weeks I was confined to bed and, having nothing better to do, I began to think about myself. Why was I in bed? Why was I in hospital? Why was I born at all? Sitting on my feet, to keep them still, I looked at my shaking arms and thought about my shaking head and my incessant dribbling. I was the perfect picture of a village fool, without being silly. I still could not walk nor could I sit on my bottom, but only insecurely on the end of my spine. I knew that I was a 'spastic' but to myself I was normal. I thought I could speak all right too, but I was not told why I was in bed.

Because of the war Mum wanted me to be evacuated to a home for handicapped children and not to go into a hospital. When Dad was alive he just would not let me go into hospital again, as he did not think that they could do anything for me. But here I was in a ward in a world that I did not know, or like very well. I was very homesick at first and cried a lot.

The cream and green ward in which I occupied a bed was for girls with heart trouble. After a while I made friends with some of them, but then they went home and I had to start again. Because of my defective speech it was not easy, but now I was happier and beginning to settle down.

After about five weeks the doctor thought she would give me a proper examination and after doing the usual things such as testing my heart (which is very good) and knocking the elbow and knee joints to see if they shoot up in the air (which of course they did), she then tested for stiffness of the muscles. There was not much stiffness, the ankles moved easily, so the next stage was to walk. I was undressed and held up under the arms by the sister who walked me naked up and down the ward. I did not mind as I was quite used to doing things like that. The doctor then announced that I had better have some treatment and get up for a while every day.

The following morning a new routine started. After breakfast I was dressed and allowed to stay up until tea-time. During the day I sat by the bed of another girl, with my legs underneath it (this was the only way that I could keep my balance) so that she could help me with my dinner, because if I fed myself most of the food was wasted. This girl also helped me to do schoolwork and I let her play with my rag doll—I did not take any china dolls into hospital. At the least excuse I was put back to

18

bed and treated as a sick person, having my temperature taken every day.

A masseuse gave me daily treatment which I liked very much. This consisted of simple exercises, massage and walking up and down, up and down the ward with the masseuse walking behind and holding me in position. She was very good to me because she had known and remembered me as a baby; I was sorry when she left.

School was held every day in the ward, but our teacher had to give lessons both to us and to the children in the adjoining ward. As they were mostly very young it was natural that she should spend most of her time with them. We were left to work with our books, and most of the girls could do quite a lot of work by themselves, but with my scanty schooling, for all the use they were to me the books might just as well have been printed in a foreign language—although it is true that some of them did have some pretty pictures.

I could read 'the cat sat on the mat' and things like that, but no more, so I was given the Beacon Reader Book 3 and that book haunted me for years! I could not read it but I was too ashamed to say so and no one ever found out because when I tried to read I dribbled profusely and swamped the book—so in self-defence the teachers left me alone. How I wished that Dad had taught me a little more of the art of reading!

Like most people Dad and Mum loved music and they had always sung popular songs while doing their household chores. I can well remember one sunny day after school I was sitting alone in the day-room, singing to myself. Suddenly a young nurse came in and asked what I was doing. 'Singing,' I said.

'I thought you were in pain,' she replied quite seriously. I did not sing again for years. You see, I was shocked because I thought I had a lovely voice.

That evening, when we were all tucked up for the night and most of the girls were asleep, I lay in bed watching the evening sun shining through the windows and playing with the shadow of the trees that grew outside, and I thought of the good day we had had playing in the courtyard outside the ward. My eyes were turned towards the big green swing doors at the end of the ward when suddenly I became conscious of a man standing there. It was the ghost of my father and he seemed to be saying, 'Don't worry, I will look after you.' When I looked again the vision had faded, but it was very real for those few minutes. I do and always will believe that Dad has helped me down the years—surely no human hand could guide so well.

When a child is at home his mother is the most important person in his life, but in hospital Mother becomes a kind of fairy godmother who comes on visiting days and brings sweets, comics and toys. I loved to see Mum, Stanley and Gladys, but I did not have a real life with them any more now that I had started to make a life of my own.

In Queen Mary's Hospital, as in most children's hospitals, it was the rule that all sweets were confiscated and evenly distributed at mealtimes. After one visiting day I had secreted a box of chocolates under my pillow and was quietly beginning to eat them in bed when the deputy matron came on her rounds. Hastily I thrust the box under the pillow, but unfortunately it broke and the precious sweets tumbled to the floor. A nurse was told to take them away; I was given a good talking to, and instantly burst into tears. As soon as the matron had gone a kind-hearted nurse returned my sweets, but ever since then, whenever I see that particular brand of chocolates, I re-live the horror of that moment.

I was now making friends more quickly and got on well with most of the girls in the ward—except for one very pretty girl and we had a mutual dislike for each other. She delighted in mocking my handicap and as at that time I had a limited sense of humour and a very bad temper, I would get very cross. One day she teased me so much that I said 'Do you want a fight?' She replied, 'O.K.,' so I knelt up in bed the best way I could to keep my balance and we began to fight. Before long I had torn a large piece out of her drill-slip, and when the sister found out I was confined to bed for a week. The girl never mocked me again, but all the same I felt very hurt because she could and did tell her version of the incident to the sister so she got off scot-free, but because I could not do so I was punished.

During those warm sunny days it was pleasant to lie on the bed and watch the birds going about their daily business high above our heads, or to sit on the grass and smell the sweet-scented air while we talked. The war seemed far away. We saw a great many aeroplanes, but that was all, until October when Hitler started dropping his bombs. One night all the children were sleeping peacefully and only the night staff were awake, when a bomb fell on the ward for spastics. Some of the children were very badly hurt and the nurse received a hip injury, but luckily no one was killed. The next day we were having our dinner when the assistant matron informed us that we were all being sent to another hospital. We were stripped of all our clothes (as these belonged to the hospital), rolled in blankets like parcels, and despatched in ambulances to an unknown destination.

Dusk was falling as the ambulances pulled up outside a long wooden building somewhere in the country and soon all the children were carried on stretchers into a dimly lit ward. There were so many of us being taken in together that we became rather mixed and I was put into a bed with a boy on one side and a baby on the other. The girls I had known at Queen Mary's were sent to another part of the hospital as our ward was full.

When we were safely in bed supper was served and some soldiers, who were patients in another part of the hospital, came in to help feed the babies and those who, like myself, could not manage alone.

Later that evening the doctors examined each of us in turn and asked what was wrong and what treatment we had been receiving. When they came to me I told them I had spastic paralysis, but they could not understand what I said although I repeated it about ten times. They were under the impression that I had chorea, which is a disease of the heart and the treatment for which is complete rest, so I was told to lie down and not move and all my protests were in vain.

For the next eight days I was allowed to do nothing but lie absolutely flat—even food and drink was taken in the supine position—and as I could not read there was plenty of time to think.

When daylight came I could look around me and out of the window I could see hills. Rolling, round, green, lovely hills. I spent many hours a day dreaming I was walking across them. The ward was built of wood; it was very long and it was full of boys and babies, with not another girl amongst them. In fact I was in a strange world where I knew no one and no one knew me or anything about me.

Soon it was visiting day and Mum came to see me and of course wondered why I was in bed and on my back; so she had a long talk with the sister and explained my handicap. Meanwhile Gladys told me where I was; it was Cuckfield Hospital, about twenty miles from Brighton and near Haywards Heath, and it really belonged to one of the big London children's hospitals. When Mum came back I said, 'Mummy, I want to get up.'

'Be a good girl,' she replied, 'they are trying a new treatment on you.'

I knew she only said this to console me; however, next morning sister had a chat with the doctor and after that I had to get up every day.

When Christmas came that year the country-side wore a white dress of snow and from the ward windows was a beautiful view of snow-capped hills. We had already seen the porters carry in a tree so big that the top had to be sawn off before there was room to stand it upright, and when we woke on Christmas morning there was great excitement as we all looked in our pillow-cases to see what presents we had been given.

That morning I was tied into a wheel-chair, so as not to fall out, and was taken to a carol service in the main part of the hospital. Everyone sang with real feeling and we were all very happy when our visitors arrived in the afternoon. The day passed much too quickly and soon Mum and Gladys had gone home, the tree was bare and the lights were out. But my locker was full and I had enjoyed this first Christmas in hospital. What if I had no friends to talk to? The boys did not want to talk to a girl and the babies cried when I looked at them. However, the nurses were very kind to me as I was the only big girl in the ward.

Soon after Christmas a number of the children went home and those who were left were sad to see the wooden hut closed. I was taken into a ward in the main building. All the children here were young and most of them were seriously ill. I had to be very quiet and spent most of the time sitting up in bed trying to draw. Sometimes I got up in the afternoons and sat by the fire in a little room with the older girls, but they did not talk much as they were seriously ill. The following days passed uneventfully and it was quite an occasion when one young girl was given a blood transfusion. I well remember the fascination of watching the blood trickle down the tube into her arm.

A few days after the blood episode the doctor came in and pushed up my nightdress sleeve to take a sample of my blood. As he was doing this I gazed up into his handsome face and fell secretly in love with him. He soon became my favourite doctor and I shall always be grateful to him for the time and energy he spent in trying to help me. He called in many other doctors to ask their opinion, and had endless consultations on 'this interesting case', but it was all in vain and I got no better.

After about a month had elapsed the wooden hut was reopened and filled with the children who had been evacuated from London. For my part I was very happy—it was much more like home in the hut than in the ward. There were a great many babies of about one-year-old, some big boys and myself. Very soon all but one of the boys was sent home. The remaining one was Bill. He was thirteen (the same age as myself) and had a very weak heart so that he had to spend most of his time lying down. As all his friends had now gone he began to talk to me and soon we became inseparable.

Before knowing Bill my letters home had always been written on foolscap sheets of paper, in block capitals about three inches high, which looked as if a spider had walked all over them, and read something like this:

Dear Mummy,

I hope you are keeping well. I have been up today. I have had a nice bath in a big bath and been put to bed.

Lots of love from
VERA.

There was never room to write more than this on one sheet of paper—even if I had known how to spell the words that I wanted to use—but now that Bill was my friend he took over the job of writing letters from my dictation. He took the trouble to understand what I said and very soon we were having long and interesting conversations together. Bill was the first real friend I ever had, he was a person to whom I could talk and ask questions. For some time we were the only two older children in the ward until one day Kathleen, who was also thirteen, was admitted, and she became the firm friend of both of us. She had a T.B. spine and had to spend all her time in bed, but even so we managed to have a great deal of fun together.

Not long after this one of the babies developed measles and the ward was put into quarantine. As soon as this baby was better another was sent away with dysentery—and so it went on. Those babies seemed to get every possible illness and as soon as a new infectious disease was diagnosed we three older children were inoculated against it. We became used to having needles pushed into our arms and legs but there is one injection which I shall never forget. I was the only one allowed up in the ward while we were in quarantine and one day, when the doctor arrived carrying in another strange-looking bottle, I remarked, 'What now? I am beginning to look like a pin-cushion!'

We soon discovered it was an injection against chicken-pox

and it was given in the buttocks. Well, it was all right for Bill and Kath, they were in bed, but I was not allowed to go to bed until after tea each day so I had to spend the rest of the time sitting on a pillow, but even then it was very painful.

One night I woke up with earache and a swollen face and everyone thought I had mumps. It was a beautiful day and all the other beds were pushed outside, but I had to stay in. I was feeling thoroughly depressed when suddenly Mum and Stanley came in. Stanley had joined the R.A.F. six months previously and this was his first leave, so of course I was terribly thrilled to see him. He was always playing the fool and could make any-one laugh, and it was not long before I had forgotten I was ill and the doctor remarked that it was the most rapid recovery from mumps that he had ever known.

A few days later Stanley came again and brought his camera with him with the intention of taking some snaps. To me a camera was an object of wonder—one of those fragile things to be looked at but not touched—but I so much wanted a snap of my big brother that I asked if I could take one. Stanley laughed and made jokes about it until he had put the magic box be-tween my knees as I knelt on the grass. He put his hat under the front of it and then ran round to lie in front of me. I grabbed the camera very tightly with both hands and both knees and, tensing every muscle in my body, I took my first snap. To me it was a tremendous achievement and that photograph has always taken pride of place in my album.

It was a glorious summer that year and we children spent most of the time on the grass outside our hut. We used to go on to an old tennis court which still had wire netting round three sides of the square. I would crawl over to this netting and look at the wonderful dog-rose that worked its way in and out, up and up. It was among those delicate little pink flowers that the grasshoppers lived. I would try to catch some of them to put into matchboxes, but I am afraid that none of those I caught survived my powerful grip long enough to see the in-side of a matchbox!

Out into the World

One day while we were outside the nurse asked Bill to give me some jelly for tea, and he put the two plates on his pillow while he knelt up to put some things on the bottom of his bed. Alas! my wayward arms shot out without warning and knocked one of the jellies all over the bed. Poor Bill! Before I could warn him he had sat in it—how we laughed! Bill had to have a clean bed.

Bill and I had a great deal of fun together but he was curious to know why I never got any better. 'I have known boys with chorea before and they have always got well and gone home,' he said. I explained, 'I am a spastic, which means that something is wrong with the way I move, but I don't know what.'

'Will you ever get better?' asked Bill.

'One day, when the war is over,' I replied confidently, 'and then I will be a great doctor and help others.'

But time was passing much too quickly for all the games we wanted to play. Our favourite one was 'dare' and this was always played at night after we had been tucked down. Usually this game consisted of throwing things over the oak beams which went across the ceiling of the hut. Once my doll became wedged there and Bill had to climb up the iron roof supports to get it back. Another time we dared Kath to get out of bed and ride the rocking-horse. Unfortunately the nurse came in, caught her and put her back to bed surrounded by screens. Directly the nurse had left, Kath was out of bed and kicked the screens down, much to our amusement. However, this exploit didn't seem to amuse the nurse and poor old Kath was in trouble again.

After eight months of this free and easy existence the doctors decided it was time we had some schooling, so a teacher was duly employed to come in for two hours daily. Under her tuition I learned the alphabet all over again, and then, for some reason or other, she didn't come any more and our lessons ceased.

Bill was now getting better and was allowed up most of the time. After various expeditions to the bottom of our field he would come back and tell me all about the wonderful things that he found there. 'Take me down there, I can walk with your help,' I would plead, but he always refused. One day, however, he came back and told me about some baby frogs he had found and I decided that I must see them for myself.

'I don't believe there are any,' I said. 'You will have to prove it by taking me there.'

'Oh, you are much too heavy,' replied Bill.

'I won't eat anything tomorrow if you will take me down in the evening,' I retorted. So it was settled, and the next evening, with the help of another boy who had joined the ward, I was given a bandy chair to that wonderful place at the end of the field. I didn't realize how tired it would make Bill and he never attempted it again.

But all good things must end and after eleven happy months in Cuckfield the doctor came in one Friday morning and said Bill and I were to go back to Queen Mary's Hospital. At ten-thirty the next morning we were put into an ambulance and off we went. We arrived after some hours on the road and were put into two beds in the admission ward without anything to show who we were and where we had come from. The sister asked Bill his name, etc., and then she asked me mine. I tried to tell her but she could not understand, so she asked Bill. He told her my name and home address and then told her I was a spastic. Sister asked three times if I was mentally deficient and three times Bill said no. When the doctor came she told him I was a spastic and as it was thought that all spastics were very backward my case papers were marked 'mentally backward'. (I know this to be true because I read it a year later.) After examination Bill was sent to a ward for heart diseases while I was taken to the ward for incurables, and with tears in my eyes I said good-bye to him and never saw him again.

3

A New Life Begins

On arrival in the ward I was put to bed and at about four o'clock in the afternoon, as I sat there playing with my teddy bear, the nurses began putting everyone else to bed. Big boys, little boys, big girls, and little girls, they were all being put to bed. It was not long before everyone was talking about me—not to me, and I felt very silly because for some unknown reason every time I tried to talk, the children would just laugh and make fun of me. I wished that Bill was there and when I was tucked down for the night I dreamt about him and forgot my unhappiness.

I was kept in bed a month and every day my bed was taken into the dayroom for school. I can well remember the teacher giving me a very small writing book with lines in it, a new pencil and Beacon Reader Book 3, in a box. The teacher said that when I got up she would help me, but that I was not to worry about it while I was in bed.

After a month of just sitting in bed I was allowed to get up. We all got up at 5.30 a.m. to give us time to dress for breakfast at eight. The nurses would wake us and give us our clothes, then dress some of the babies before helping us. I did try to dress myself, but never managed more than my knickers and drill-slip as I was so afraid of falling off the bed.

All the big children were dressed by about six-thirty and then we used to go into the dayroom to play. Very often one of the children would disagree with another and then there would be civil war. The one who had disagreed would get all her friends together and the two sides would have a real fight until someone came in to stop us, when we would all kiss and make up. One morning I did something which no one agreed with, so I was put into a spare wheel-chair and left at the back of an empty ward with the back wheel down a hole. I was not missed until breakfast time and that morning taught me not to join in other people's arguments.

Breakfast, dinner or tea, it made no difference. Bibs were put on us, but there were not enough nurses to feed us all so we had to feed ourselves and the food went everywhere. When we did not like our food it would go on the floor or the ceiling. I wonder how we kept alive because not much of our food went inside us.

When I was in bed I had longed to get up and sit at the long table with all the other children; but now that I was up there was not enough room for me, so I had to sit in one small chair with a bigger one in front of me for my books. This was not a very good idea because the chair I used as a table moved every time I tried to write and I dribbled all the while. I did try to do my lessons, but I wondered why the teacher never marked my work. One day she told the class to write out the well-known poem 'Trees'. I thought that if I wrote this all right she would mark it and be pleased. It took me a month to do, and it was very hard work which I did not enjoy. Every day I hung the bit I had done over the fireguard to dry—it was so wet with dribble. When I had finished the teacher did not mark it because she could not understand my scribble. I was so hurt that I did not worry about school for a long time.

After tea, at about four o'clock, we were put to bed and it was this time of the day that I liked best. I could sit up in bed with restrainers (long tapes) tied on to stop me falling over, and could then draw or sew or play with the girl in the next bed. Sewing was done with a bodkin, as a needle was too dangerous, and it was hard work as the material became rather messy by the time I had finished with it. About five o'clock the nurse used to come and take our temperatures and then we had supper and were tucked down for the night.

Not all the children in the ward were spastics, some were just mentally deficient—one little girl went around saying to everyone, 'Love me, kiss me.' Some had polio and wore long irons and there was one boy who had a wasting disease. He used to sit in his wheel-chair and write everybody's letters, or sometimes the other boys would take him to play with them. Laurence, for that was his name, did not have much time for the girls, but I am afraid all the girls ran after him. He was such a handsome boy that even I admired him. Whenever we found ourselves alone he would tell me about his family, or if I got into trouble I used to go to him and tell him about it and he would help.

Of the spastics some were weak and stiff, some were very stiff, some could not keep still and some had epileptic fits. There was one very small boy called Brian who could do nothing for himself and used to go around in a walking-chair, until he had an operation to uncross his legs after which he stayed in bed. There was Rita, the little girl who slept next to me so that I could call the nurse when she had a fit in her sleep. We were not classed as mentally deficient because we were not certified, but everyone thought we were not quite right in the head.

We did have some treatment. Some of us were taken to another ward three times a week for drill. This ward was fitted up like a gym with wall bars, parallel bars, couches and all that kind of thing. The young masseuses would walk us up and down and give us simple exercises. Then they would take our boots off, put their hands under our feet and push. This hurt very much, but if anyone cried with pain they were spoken to sharply by another masseuse. I will never forget the look on some of the children's faces when they had their feet stretched.

Because most of the children had been in hospital since they were babies and knew nothing of the outside world, their games were based on hospital life. They did not know what a train or a pram was because they had never seen one; they did not know what a shop was, so how could they play at shopping? They could only talk about things that went on in hospitals, and it is true to say that they lived in a world of their own, but this was because they knew no other life and not because they were silly.

Because of my bad speech and because I had lived at home until I was twelve, the other children did not always understand me and when they did they did not always believe me because I talked of a world they did not know. I was called the 'know-all' and except for talking a little with Laurie I grew very quiet and often played by myself. The ward sister had told me off once or twice for little things, and once she had put me to bed when I accidentally threw a cup at Rita. Poor girl, I gave her a black eye and nobody believed my story which was that I went to give her back her empty cup but could not reach her, so I gave a little shove, but my shove was too hard and anyway I wobbled. After that I grew very timid and always tried to be very good.

One day we had a new boy in the ward; a weak little thing who could not keep still. He could not talk to anybody because he could not open his mouth very wide. The sister used to let him sit in her office and read, and she forbade some of us to go near him in case he might get hurt. His name was John—'My John' as people call him to this day, and he was going to play a very big part in my life in the years to come. It does seem funny now to think that at one time I was not allowed to play with him.

After I had been on the ward a little while I got tired of just sitting at the table all day long, so I asked sister if I could use a walking-chair. The only spare one was rather small and was a three-sided affair with three wheels on the bottom, a very small tray in front and a saddle of webbing to sit on, which made me so sore that I took it off. I did not know how much harm I was doing to myself, so I used to go everywhere in this monstrosity, dribbling all the time. I used to lean over the top rather far because the more I leaned the faster and better I could go.

One day, near the end of a school holiday, we were all playing in the courtyard when a nurse came and told us to line up against the wall as a new doctor was coming round. When the doctor came to me he took one look at my hands, which were resting on the tray of the chair, and said, 'How long have you had all these warts?'

I told him I had had them since I was a little girl and that all the treatment I had had did not get rid of them. He asked if I would let him cut them out and it was arranged that in a fort-night's time he should give me a local anaesthetic and remove some of them. On the day of the operation I was so frightened that the knife would slip and cut off my thumb that sweat and tears poured down my face and I was glad when he had finish-ed. But afterwards I wished the doctor had cut off all the warts as both my hands were covered with the ugly things.

Not long after this I was in school one day, almost asleep, when the sister said that we were moving to another ward right at the back of the hospital, on the orders of the new medical superintendent. For the next week we were all kept in bed while everything was packed up and then we were taken, in our beds, to our new home. This ward was much more shut in and I am afraid that none of the children liked it very much as it was built on a hill. We could not get out on to the grass because the hill went steeply up behind the ward and down in front. The sister left and we had another one who liked to keep us clean and tidy, so we did not get up very much—anyway, I was always being put to bed with colds and such-like. Then another teacher came and she thought we were 'poor little things' and told us stories all day.

In the late summer of 1942 John, Laurie and I became good friends. We had a lot in common and we used to talk and play together by the hour. Laurie loved to hear about the out-side world. He could play the piano wonderfully and would play anything we asked for. John read a lot. I did not have many friends at this time and when the two boys wanted to play on their own I felt very hurt and unwanted as the other children did not want to play with the 'dribbler' or the 'know-all'.

It was because of this dull life that after visiting time one day near Christmas I told sister that Mother wanted me to have an operation on my weak ankles. I knew this was a lie, but I thought it would make some excitement and it was arranged that after Christmas I should see the medical superintendent. I was nearly fifteen by this time and knew that I had only one more year at Queen Mary's Hospital after which I would have to go to a woman's hospital. But for how long? Until the war was over, or for life? I did not know. I wondered why I was born, what purpose there was in living. Would it not be better to kill me, as Hitler was killing the Jews in Germany?

As I lay in bed on the last night of 1942 I thought of all the things I would do if I were normal. In my wildest dreams—and some of them were wild—I never got anywhere near the truth of what was to happen. God had His eye on me I felt sure and His will would be done, but at that time I knew, or thought I knew, that I would never get any better and so I did not want to live.

Mum had given me a game of rubber draughts for Christmas and for a week one half of the children in the ward had been saying that John was the best player while the other half said that I could beat him any day; so it was arranged that we should have a tournament at 10.30 a.m. on New Year's Day, 1943. We were sitting on the floor of the day-room, with two small children to move the draughts for us, as we were both too shaky to make our own moves. The rest of the children sat around watching intently. John and I played as if our lives depended on the outcome of the match—we each wanted to be the better man.

At eleven o'clock sister walked briskly into the room followed by a small, dark-haired woman in her thirties. We were all so engrosed in the game that we ignored her for about five minutes until the dark-haired lady interrupted us by saying, 'Which of you is Vera Dean?'

'I am,' I replied, and with those few words my whole life was changed. With one hand held firmly at the back of my neck she helped me up from the floor and said 'March!'

No one had ever spoken to me in that way before and I was so surprised that I simply did as I was bid while her hand behind my neck helped me to balance. In what seemed to be no more than a few seconds we arrived at the Separation Room, or Sep. —a small room next door to the ward. As we went I called confidentially back to John, 'I won't be long.'

The Sep. was a very small room, about 10 feet square, and its furniture consisted of a leather couch covered by a red blanket, a blue wicker armchair, another chair and a small table with a drawer. The strange woman sat me in the armchair and said, 'Please get undressed. By the way, my name is Collis, and I am going to examine you.'

I tried hard to get undressed but found this too difficult to manage alone. Mrs. Collis watched my efforts and then lent me a helping hand and put me on the slippery couch underneath the window.

'Let go,' she said soothingly, and I wondered what she meant. I looked up at her and shyly asked, 'What do you mean, please?'

She showed me with her hands how to go floppy and loose as when you are about to go to sleep. Of course, the more I tried to 'let go' the more I shook. Then Mrs. Collis produced a metronome and listening to its beat helped to take my thoughts off my shaking body. After a while she helped me to move my arms about. It all seemed so strange and so unlike what I had been used to that I began to wonder if she were not a little mad, but her hands were strong yet gentle, and she used them in such a certain way that I could not help trying to do what she told me.

Now it was dinner-time and it seemed that she must surely let me go back to the day-room, but no, she brought my dinner from the kitchen and set it out nicely on the little table, complete with a clean white tablecloth. She sat me up at the table and said, 'Enjoy your dinner.'

I picked up the spoon with my left hand; a nice bit of potato in the first spoonful went up to the ceiling, the next went on the floor. Out of about six spoonfuls about one reached my mouth, I was so scared of kicking over the table or of giving Mrs. Collis a blow in the face. It was obvious to her that if I continued at this rate the dinner would soon be gone and I would still be hungry, so she helped me with the rest of the meal, holding my hand and arm to steady them and guiding the spoon to my mouth.

Mrs. Collis left at about two o'clock and then I was allowed to go back to the day-room. John and Laurie had been really worried and greeted me with, 'Where have you been all this time? We could not hear any noise so we thought the woman had killed you!'

I told them what I had been doing and they both thought that Mrs. Collis sounded a little touched in the head. 'Do you know, Vera, if you had been in there much longer, John and I would have come and fetched you,' said Laurie, with real conviction. But I told them that there was something about Mrs. Collis which I liked, although I could not tell yet what it was, and we went on with the game of draughts which John won. I could not concentrate on the game, my mind kept going back to that morning. Did it really happen or was it all a dream?

At this point I would like to give a few details of the history of cerebral palsy work in England, although, of course, it was some years before I knew all the facts and could piece them together. We read about palsy in the Bible when St. Matthew speaks of a man saying 'Lord, my servant lieth at home sick of the palsy and grievously tormented.' We do not know exactly what was meant.

About a hundred years ago Dr. Little made some very clever observations about certain groups of handicapped children who, it is now known, were suffering from cerebral palsy. However, he was a busy man and did not have time to study these children as much as he would have liked. The name 'Little's Disease' was introduced into medical language, but beyond this not much interest was taken and the subject was largely forgotten until 1919. At this time some doctors in America became interested and gradually showed people that something could be done to help those suffering from what they called 'cerebral palsy'. For some reason or other the word 'spastic' has come to be used here for this condition, but it is not really a very good word as it only means 'stiff' and not all people with cerebral palsy are stiff. On the other hand 'cerebral palsy' is a better term as it means 'movement difficulty coming from the brain' and that is exactly what the various handicaps included in this group are.

Mrs. Collis took her two small daughters to America at the beginning of the war to be left there for the duration, and it was while she was there that she met, through a friend, Dr. Phelps who had an institute for cerebral-palsied children. She had always been interested in the study of movement and its development so she went to work with Dr. Phelps; and when she decided that she must return to England, he asked her if she would try to do work for the cerebral-palsied in this country. Mrs. Collis thought that it would be very difficult to start anything new in a country whose whole energy was given to fighting a war, but she said that she would try and so she sailed for England leaving her two daughters with kind Americans.

When she got home it was as she feared. She talked to many doctors and authorities all over the country, but everyone was so busy with the war that they did not have the time or the energy to investigate the subject. However, at last one doctor did listen to her and, although he thought it a bit peculiar that anyone should want to work with what he considered to be hopeless cases, he agreed to let her try out her ideas at Queen Mary's Hospital, and she started there on the 1st January 1943, the day she and I first met.

A New Life Begins

I think Mrs. Collis's study and research into the problems of cerebral palsy have shown that something goes wrong with voluntary movement, for movement as well as thought comes from the brain and the two are inseparable. Many people have joined in the work since she started and they all use the same words to mean different things. As everyone knows, movement originates in the brain—the brain sends out messages to various parts of the body and in a normal person these messages are automatically obeyed. The important thing to remember is that in cerebral palsy it is from the brain that things go wrong, and not one or more parts of the body or muscles that are affected. Also, each cerebral-palsied person is different from all the others—I know plenty of children and adults with this handicap and no two of them are absolutely alike, although they can be broadly divided into groups or types.

Of course, Mrs. Collis, like everyone else, had to start from the beginning. She has tried many ways and many different things to help the handicapped child. She discards that which is not helpful and builds upon that which proves good, so that treatment today is much simpler and yet more effective than it was in 1943. She has also shown the best way of helping these people is for their handicap to be diagnosed in infancy so that their upbringing can be managed from the beginning with regard to their difficulty. The cerebral-palsied person has got to be helped and shown how to move in a way that is different from that which comes naturally to him. People who understand his problem can help him with this as he cannot manage it on his own. On the other hand, nobody can move for him—this he must do for himself, and nobody can speak for him either. Mrs. Collis often repeated this to me as she was showing me how to make good use of my limited function. It must be remembered that for the cerebral-palsied person even a very simple act may be as difficult as walking on a tight-rope would be for most normal people. It is always important that an atmosphere of serenity and concentration should prevail when the child is trying to learn how to live—and that means all the time.

4

Setbacks and Tears

The day came when I was taken to the medical superintendent for an examination in connection with the proposed operation on my ankles. I had no fear of this as I thought it would do some good. While the examination was in progress Mrs. Collis talked to the superintendent and gave him her reasons against surgery for cerebral palsy. Surgery had always been one of the orthodox treatments given, but Mrs. Collis was so convincing in her arguments against it that I was handed back to her with the words, 'Take this child and do what you like with her.'

The superintendent knew that Mrs. Collis was approaching the problem from a special point of view and he asked her if, in addition to the five children she was then treating each day, she would also see what she could do for John.

John was not very keen on this idea as he had formed a bad opinion of all medical people and he objected to being undressed—not so much from shyness as from a feeling that it was all a sheer waste of time. However, in the months that followed, he became very fond of Mrs. Collis and always tried to do as she asked.

After the first and very difficult year quite a number of children had passed through Mrs. Collis's hands. Her method of recruitment was to make a tour of the other wards in the hospital and when she found a child she thought she could help, that child was transferred to her care. If the child proved to be too mentally limited then he or she was transferred back again.

It soon became apparent that the best results were achieved with the youngest children and so the day came when Laurie, John and I were the only older children left. In order to convince the authorities Mrs. Collis had to prove that children could be helped so she had to choose those who would soonest show the result of her help.

John did not like this arrangement, as previously there had been a number of big boys to be his friends and now he felt alone, as I had done for so long. So one day he came to me and with his left hand holding his mouth open, said:

'Vera, will you be my best friend now that everybody has left? Laurie is so ill that I have nobody to play with.'

It was in this childish way that John and I became friends; a friendship that has lasted to this day. For a long time I had wondered why the doctors were so interested in John's handicap and one day he told me his sad story.

John was a normal baby; he lived with his mother and grandmother in a small house at a busy holiday resort on the east coast of England. When he was seven years old he had severe whooping cough followed by diphtheria. The cough was so bad that in some way it damaged his brain and he became cerebral-palsied. At his local hospital it was not known what was wrong with him and he was sent to a famous teaching hospital in London. At this time the air-raids were very severe and gradually John became worse. His spine was bent sideways so that when he tried to walk his right hand reached the ground. At other times his right arm just curled up and he could not use it. He had great difficulty in speaking and eating since he could open his mouth no more than an inch. He was handicapped in all parts of his body and shook from head to toe during all his waking hours.

The doctors in London found they could do nothing so they sent John to Queen Mary's, where every night he was made to sleep in a plaster boat in an effort to straighten his spine. When he was strapped in he could not move so he could not sleep and often he had to be doped. Many times I woke in the night and heard him crying. It took John years to accept his handicap and the loneliness of being away from his mother. To go home was his one and only aim in life until Mrs. Collis came along. She never allowed him to sleep in the boat or to wear a plaster jacket, and under her guidance he worked hard and improved a great deal.

As the scope of Mrs. Collis's influence grew so also did the opposition to her work. This was because, though she was fully qualified in her work and had done much medical study, her ideas were out of keeping with traditional treatment and the other people saw only that she did not keep to tradition. Most of them did not mind what she did so long as she did not interfere with them, but one or two were more difficult and would try to cause trouble. However, she understood the reasons for their behaviour and always managed to appear calm even when she wasn't.

Individual work in the treatment room went on every day, and after I had learned to stop struggling over everything I did I was taught to sit on my buttocks and not on the base of my spine. The next thing was to tighten my tummy and buttocks and kneel up in front of a mirror. This took a lot of concentration, but gradually it became easier and one day I remarked to Mrs. Collis that I wished I could dance, although I did not know much about ballet and had never seen one. This gave her an idea and she obtained an old gramophone and some records of 'Swan Lake' so that when I knelt in front of the mirror I could be a little swan, dancing with my arms in time to the rhythm of the music. We both loved dancing and when life got a bit hectic (as it often did) Mrs. Collis would put on a record and sit in the armchair while I knelt and danced for her. Like this we could both forget the jealousies and struggles that were going on around us.

I was still so shaky that I could use no toys except a big box of bricks, and with these I built high chimneys, long trains and good bridges. If John knocked them down before I had finished I would get very angry. I played with bricks not because I was mentally backward but because this sort of thing should be part of every child's early life and as I had missed it in babyhood it seemed exciting to me at a much later stage than is usual.

One cold wet afternoon in March 1943 we were all examined to see if we had made any progress. The slippery couch in the 'Sep.' had been replaced by a plain wooden table covered with blankets, and as I was placed on it one of the doctors said, 'This child will never be able to stand alone.'

To prove this he picked me up under the arms and stood me on the floor waiting to catch me as I fell, but to the complete surprise of everyone, including myself, I stood unsupported for about a minute. For the first time in my fifteen years I had stood alone without support and it was as if a miracle had happened. Mrs. Collis went very white and had to sit down, then in a voice which rose almost from a whisper to a cry of triumph, she said, 'I never thought Vera was going to stand so soon; and I do believe that one day she will walk. It might take years, but she will do it. Already she can feed and dress herself.' Then, for the second time in three months, she was told to take me and do what she could with me.

The next morning Mrs. Collis asked if I wanted to be able to walk by myself, to which I replied that of course I did, so after the routine work I began to learn to stand properly. At first I could stand only for a few seconds and it was really hard work, but after a while it was possible to keep it up for five or ten minutes and I used to go to the corner of the room and watch the other children working. I stood there not because I was naughty but because if I tumbled backwards the wall would stop me from falling to the ground. Unfortunately it became such a habit to stand in the corner that for a while I could not stand anywhere else. Sometimes I stood there for a whole morning, and by noon my legs ached so much that I was glad to sit down to dinner.

Mrs. Collis always had her dinner sent up from the kitchen and ate with us. She did not take milk pudding and always gave it to me. I looked forward to having dinner with her as she would talk to me about anything and everything; she was like a big sister. Unlike everybody else, she encouraged me to speak my mind and say what I felt. There are many people in this world who think that because you have a handicap you have nothing to say; but this is not so, as people who have taken the trouble to listen have often discovered.

Mrs. Collis did not have any assistants to help her and had to do everything herself. Since no one was able to understand my speech we worked at this on Saturday mornings. Seated in front of a mirror I would watch her lips and try to copy the sounds she made. I spent so much time looking into a mirror in those days that now I can hardly face one! It was essential that I should speak clearly because I was spending several hours each day in the treatment room; Mrs. Collis said I was her right hand, and asked me to help her in many ways.

By now there was a need for someone to do carpentry and Mr. Grant, who worked in the hospital splint shop, was transferred to the ward. His first job was to make me a pair of skis, similar to real skis but shorter, more clumsy and made from wood. These were strapped to my boots and prevented me from crawling about. I no longer used the walking-chair as it had already been responsible for creating certain posture faults, so, for the time being, I was unable to move about alone.

Gradually I learned to walk with the skis and then began the task of learning to walk without them. Mr. Grant made me a support called 'the crab', which can best be described as a three-legged walking-stick made of steel. This I pushed in front while Mrs. Collis walked behind talking all the time about a variety of subjects, or else making up silly poems like this: ' "Walk a little faster," said Vera to the crab, "there's a woman just behind me playing snatch and grab." ' Now I cannot look at a real crab without thinking of that and wanting to laugh.

Besides making things to be used in the treatment room Mr. Grant made, or adapted, most of our toys. He put a big fat handle on a doll's pram so that Rita could grip it and push it about. I thought this was a good idea until one day I put the china doll, which Mum had brought me a few weeks previously, in the pram and it tipped up because the handle was so heavy. The doll fell out and broke. John buried it at the back of the field and I cried myself to sleep that night.

Another toy made by Mr. Grant was a catapult and it gave a great deal of fun to John and me. We collected pieces of wood and tried to shoot them over the roof, but one lovely summer day we shot a piece of wood straight through a linen window (the glass window had previously been broken by bomb-blast and had been replaced by a piece of linen). We were so frightened that John hid the catapult and then put a big toy rabbit on the window-sill to cover the hole in the linen. He waited until the night nurse came on duty and then asked her to stick a piece of sticking plaster over the hole so that our crime would not be discovered.

Time was passing and although we were all improving under our new treatment most people still thought we were silly. In order to settle the matter a psychiatrist came down from County Hall and examined us one by one. I was asked to read to her and, because of my scanty education, was given a very simple children's book, which I read with great difficulty. Then the psychiatrist asked me to do some simple sums such as 2 plus 4 or 12 plus 10, and then 2 subtracted from 6 or 9 from 33. This was followed by some ordinary general knowledge questions. Later she told Mrs. Collis that I was intelligent but that I needed schooling, and she added that poor speech was one of my biggest handicaps. All this made Mrs. Collis even more determined to show people that normally intelligent cerebral-palsied people could, with the right help, become useful citizens and take their rightful places in life.

My brother had been sent to India with the R.A.F. and had endured many privations and hardships, so I was overjoyed one day when he turned up out of the blue to see me. When he joined the R.A.F. he volunteered for flying duties, but somehow his papers had been muddled and he had been sent to

India with the ground staff. When the mistake was discovered he was drafted back to England for further training to achieve his ambition to become a wireless operator in a pathfinder squadron.

Stanley had beautiful blue eyes and perfect eyesight—he could see almost as well in the dark as most people can in daylight. He had a talent for drawing and painting, and his letters were always illustrated with funny little pictures. No matter how depressing his surroundings he could always find something to laugh about and everyone liked to read his cheery letters.

It was no wonder that on his now frequent visits to the hospital he received a rousing welcome from staff and patients alike. He would act the fool in such an easy way that everyone rocked with laughter. Several nurses asked me to put in a good word with him for them, but he would not be serious with anyone and as he was fond of good food he always courted the cooks at the camps at which he was stationed.

At this time not many people believed in Mrs. Collis, but I think that Stanley was one of the first people in England to realize that she knew what she was talking about. In January 1944, I received a letter from him which ended as follows:

'How are you getting on with your new arrangement, "the crab"? Gladys has told me what it looks like, I hope you are finding it helps you along. Mrs. Collis is certainly doing all she can for you but a lot is up to you, so you will have to try very hard because when the war is over I want to see you standing in Whitehall waving to us as we go by in the victory procession. So start trying very hard as it won't be long now. Give Mrs. Collis my thanks for all she is doing.'

Apart from a greetings telegram on my birthday a few days later, this letter was the last I heard from Stan. My grandmother had been dead only a fortnight when on the 28th January, 1944, Mother received a telegram to say that Stanley had been killed during the previous night while on a training flight. It was to have been almost the last practice flight for him

44

and his crew before he was due to come home for a fortnight's leave as a fully fledged sergeant wireless operator. We discovered later that a stray German fighter had penetrated our defences, and finding an unarmed training plane had shot it down with its crew of five, who had all been instantly killed. The news was such a shock to Mum that she has never quite recovered. She could not understand why God took him and not me. He was strong and healthy and, really, what good was I in life?

Gladys told me the terrible news on Saturday afternoon; and sister must have rung up Mrs. Collis for she came in on the Sunday morning, a thing she rarely did, specially to see me. At the time I felt very numb and did not want to see her, but we talked for a long time and she told me that now both my father and brother were dead she would be a friend to me. Much more than someone who just wanted to help my handicap—a real friend. Her parting words were, 'You will need someone to help you in the future, someone outside your family. Please Vera, may I be that someone? I would like to help you for what you are, not for what you might have been or for what you will never be, but for what you are now; I know better than anyone else how great your handicap is.'

5

I Learn to Talk

Life must go on for the living and it did for me. The shock of
Stan's death made my handicap much worse than it had been,
although I did not realize this at the time. All my old shakiness
returned and Mrs. Collis had to work twice as hard to prevent
her previous efforts from being wasted. However, time is a
great healer and gradually it became clear to me that the last
thing Stan would have wanted me to do would have been to
grieve for him, and as the effects of the shock lessened I tried
once again to make something worthwhile of my life.

For a long time Mrs. Collis had said to John and me, 'When
you two can feed yourselves I will take you out to tea,' and at
last, one lovely spring day, the great occasion arrived. There
was a certain amount of red tape to be cut because it was against
all the rules of the hospital to allow patients outside the gates.
It was feared that we might catch some kind of infectious
disease—although when one thinks of this it is really rather
funny considering that, although no one had been allowed out
before, our ward was almost always in quarantine.

When permission was granted we were taken by car to Dean
Farm, a really lovely old-fashioned farmhouse where, for our
tea, we had cake of any sort we liked. This was a tremendous
treat as cake in hospital in war-time was rarely seen. After tea
we went to the house in Chipstead Valley where Mrs. Collis
had a furnished room, and I could not help thinking what a nice
bed she had; it looked so soft and comfortable and different

from the hard hospital ones. Then, as it was such a warm and sunny afternoon, John and I picked some flowers from the garden and sat and watched the traffic on the nearby road. This to us was wonderful. I had not seen a bus or pram for three years and very few cars came into the hospital. We would have sat there and watched it all for hours, but soon the time came for us to return to the hospital and two tired, happy children went to bed to dream of the wonderful outside world.

During all this time there was a struggle going on between Mrs. Collis, who wanted to see us treated as ordinary people with a special difficulty, and those members of the hospital staff who were trained to look after sick children and would have preferred to have kept us in bed all the time, so that our wards could be kept clean and tidy. People like this did not mind Mrs. Collis giving us 'treatment' in special places and at special times, but did not want the usual hospital routine interfered with. This was not the way in which Mrs. Collis intended to work—it was no use her teaching us how to do things for ourselves if we were not given a chance to use our knowledge— and so there were often arguments and an uncomfortable atmosphere. My idea of happiness was to be up and doing as much as possible, but most of the time I was kept in bed with restrainers on. These, as I have mentioned, were wide pieces of tape by which we were strapped to the bed to prevent us from falling out, and it was a rule in our ward that all the children must wear them. Sometimes there were unnecessarily wet beds since a child could not get out because he was under restraint. I hated the things, and after a great deal of argument permission was at last given for me not to wear them; and with this extra freedom of movement I slept much more comfortably.

The ward doctor at this time was a very pleasant young lady who unfortunately had a bad stammer. One day as she came into the treatment room, Mrs. Collis said, 'You know, Vera, if the doctor stops to think now and again, her stammer gets much less.' This was true, and after the doctor had learnt to think about how she spoke her speech improved a great deal. On this

47

particular occasion the doctor turned to me and said, 'Do you want a job? In this basket is the skeleton of half a man. Do you think you could put him together?'

It was great fun. I laid the pieces out on the floor and put the bones together like a jigsaw puzzle until they were all in the right order. It seemed a wonderful thing to do and I was learning how the human body works.

One of the children who was transferred from another part of the hospital to our ward was Kate. She was twelve years old at the time and I was told she would be a friend for me, but Kate did not want me as a friend. The only one she wanted was John. I did not like this idea at all. How dare she take him away from me? She could not help him as I could and she could not understand what he said. But it was not long before I knew that to John, Kate was just another girl in the ward. He used to make up to her all the week long so that on Sunday, when her visitors came and brought her a small attaché-case full of sweets and cakes, she would give him half. These he put into a bag until Kate went to bed and then John and I (who always went to bed last) had a good feed. The more she imagined she made me jealous, the more sweets she gave to John. Poor Kate never knew I always had my share!

Kate had a great desire to be confirmed and after a lot of discussion she and John, Laurie and I decided we would all be confirmed together.

Our confirmation classes were given by the Reverend Dean and I could not help wondering whether he was a distant relative of mine. He was a handsome man and reminded me of my father.

The ward was in quarantine for chicken-pox on the day arranged for our confirmation and so the service had to be held in the day-room instead of the hospital chapel. John and Laurie were dressed in smart grey suits while Kate and I wore long white dresses, borrowed from the storeroom. Kate sat with Laurie, John and I sat together at the other side of the altar while a small congregation of parents and staff filled the room.

I Learn to Talk

Laurie was allowed to get up for the service and was sitting in a wheel-chair. I looked at him, so pale and thin, and then my gaze fell upon John. He looked so nice sitting there. He had become a very dear friend to me and I could not help wondering what it would be like to get married. Then the bishop walked in and we started the service. As we sang the first hymn Hitler started dropping his V.1s and they fell all round the hospital. We said our prayers to a background of explosions and finished our little service by singing that lovely hymn 'O Jesus I have promised'. When we came to the last verse and the words:

> *My hope to follow duly*
> *Is in Thy strength alone.*
> *O guide me, call me, draw me,*
> *Uphold me to the end,*

my mind went back to the time not so long ago, before I knew Mrs. Collis, when life was not very kind. I knew I could not always have her by my side and as I sang these words I realized how much strength and guidance I would need from above.

Our service concluded and the bombs kept falling long after our mothers had gone home and we had all been put to bed, but luckily none of them fell in the hospital grounds.

Not long after our confirmation Laurie was taken ill with pneumonia. At about nine o'clock, one dark winter night, the nurse woke me and said, 'Let me put you in a wheel-chair and take you in the Sep. Laurie is calling for you and I am afraid it might be too late in the morning.'

Half asleep I was wrapped warmly in blankets and was taken to his little room. In the dim light the slim pale boy looked almost like a ghost as he sat propped up in bed. He was very weak, but he smiled and talked for about half an hour before he fell into a sound sleep.

Laurie did not die that night or any other night while John and I were around. We sat by his bed day after day just talking, talking, talking; but Laurie got up only once again in his short life. Time and time again he would say 'I wish I knew someone like Mrs. Collis who would help me. Now that I know her I do like her. If only she could help me.'

If John and I went for a walk through the hospital grounds, or went for treatment, we would tell Laurie where we were going and how long we would be away. Somehow our friendship for each other seemed to give him something to live for and when at last he was moved away to one of the big London hospitals, his small spark of life just flickered out. In all the years we were together I do not remember Laurie's mother once coming to see him. I am sure she did not know what a wonderful son she had. When Mum came to see me Laurie always asked for her as he used to like to imagine she was his mother too.

When the ward was in quarantine and we were all kept in bed it was a big headache for Mrs. Collis to know how to keep us fully occupied. It was all right in term time, but at weekends and during school holidays we became very bored. It is very bad to leave a cerebral-palsied child with nothing to do. Like all children he has an active mind, but unlike a normal child he cannot do things for himself. When we were up, if one of us dropped anything someone else would pick it up, but when everybody was in bed there was no one to retrieve our toys and soon everything was on the floor and we had nothing to play with.

One morning Mrs. Collis was so tired of seeing us just sitting there doing nothing that she asked John if he would like a job. She brought some rubber sheeting from the bathroom and wrapped it around John, in his bed, leaving only his head and arms uncovered. Then she found some black varnish and asked him to varnish a picture frame. Mrs. Collis told him to try to do this without tensing more than he could help and as he was at the stage where he was still very shaky unless he was actually tightening his muscles against it, he naturally made an awful mess. Inky black varnish went everywhere, but he varnished the picture frame all right and was just about to start on the sides of his fracture board (a wooden board which was placed between the mattress and the bed spring) when the sister walked in. Horrified, she took all the things away and told John how much worse he had become lately. This, of course, was not true, but the funny thing was that we were all allowed up the next day and were not kept in bed again when the ward went into quarantine.

One of the worst things that anybody can do to a person with cerebral palsy is to tell him that he is getting worse. It has a very bad effect psychologically and will make him very self-conscious. If he is getting worse the important thing is to find out why and then put it right. But if he is just being lazy he should be told to do better. It is good policy to praise the child occasionally as this gives an incentive to do even better.

We all had fracture boards on our beds and presumably they were put there to straighten our spines, but they proved to be ineffective because most cerebral-palsied children are quite normal in sleep (and therefore the board is not required) and the actual curvature, if there is one, is usually caused by bad posture during the daytime.

During 1944 the authorities at County Hall realized that unless we were helped to overcome our speech difficulties people would always think we were silly and treat us as such. They therefore sent us a speech therapist, Miss Wood. She was very fond of poetry and would write out verses in a book and mark all the sounds that I could not say properly. The first poem I learnt was called 'Windy Night', and when it had been marked with the sounds I failed to express it looked like this:

> *Whe*ne*ver* the *moo*n *a*nd the s*ta*rs *are* s*e*t,
>   *Whe*never the *wi*nd *i*s h*igh*,
> *All* n*igh*t l*o*ng *in* the *da*rk *a*nd the *we*t,
>   *A ma*n goes *ri*ding *by*.
> L*a*te *in* the n*igh*t *w*hen the *fire*s *are* o*u*t,
>   *Why does* he gallo*p a*nd gallo*p abou*t?

I Learn to Talk

Whenever the trees are crying aloud,
  And ships are tossed at sea,
By on the highway low and loud,
  By at a gallop goes he.
By at the gallop he goes, and then
  By he comes back at the gallop again.

From this it is apparent how bad my speech was and how difficult it was for me to make conversation if I left out all the sounds I could not say clearly. It was not easy trying to concentrate in the middle of the ward, especially when we were in quarantine and Miss Wood had to sit by the bed while all the other children were noisily playing. But there was nowhere else to go as all the small rooms were occupied. I often wonder how my speech improved, but with Miss Wood's help it did.

By now all the children under Mrs. Collis used to take it in turns to have dinner with her once a week. The other children had their dinner in the day-room at a long table. I sat at the end of it to keep an eye on everybody and to start the grace. Our table was not like an ordinary one; we all had our own food trays. These were pieces of wood with two holes in them, one for the plate and one for the cup, and the trays were clamped to the table so that when the plate and cup were put in them they would not move about. Our spoons had big wooden handles so that we could hold them easily and only those children who really needed them wore bibs.

Every Monday afternoon we had a drum and tambourine band session. The real purpose of this was to teach us something about rhythm in music. In a tune that had 2 or 3 beats in a bar we would beat our drums on 1 and wait quietly on 2 and 3. If the teacher played a tune on the piano with 4 beats in the bar, we would beat our drums on 1 and 3. This was followed by singing, first in a group then individually. Some of the children had good voices, although there were others, like myself, who made a noise more like a foghorn. Our handicap made it difficult to control the volume and range of our voices and the noises we emitted varied from shrieks to grunts. Sometimes John would conduct our band and I would lead the children in a simple ballet routine. They could dance with their arms even if they could not do so with their legs. We all liked the band because like normal children we delighted in making a noise.

Although we enjoyed ourselves on Mondays we did so much more on Fridays when we had eurhythmy. We used to lie quietly on the floor and then do some simple movements to a tune on the piano. Then we pretended to dress, feed or wash ourselves, and after this we played as rabbits and crawled all over the floor. We never worried how dirty we became and were always sorry when the session ended.

Queen Mary's is a children's hospital and I knew that at the age of sixteen I would have to be transferred elsewhere. Inquiries were made throughout the country to find a training college for the physically handicapped where I could go for further education and to learn a trade, but in 1944 there was not one place that would take a girl with cerebral palsy. Nobody wanted the 'spastic' child. If I had had poliomyelitis or tuberculosis, or if I had been mentally deficient, it would have been easy. But I was born with cerebral palsy and the difficulty I had in moving would last to a certain extent till I died; therefore I could not be trained. If I had been blind or deaf or dumb it would have been all right—but no, I had cerebral palsy and nothing was offered to people like me. I could not help being as I was, and I was desperate. I felt hurt, so deeply hurt that no one was prepared to help me to make the most of my life. I knew that I was backward for my age—at sixteen I could read and write very little; this was because I had not had the chance to learn. I longed to go to college and prove my sanity.

One morning in the treatment room Mrs. Collis had to admit that she could find no training college that would have me because I was so badly handicapped and I made up my mind then and there that I would do everything in my power to help other people with the same handicap. I had ideas about helping them towards independence and giving them the chance that I had never had. If they could only learn to feed, wash and dress themselves that would be something, and I would train them for a job. It would not matter what the job was so long as they could earn a little money and feel independent. But realizing that before I could help others I had a long way to go myself, I nevertheless determined never to forget my purpose. In front of John I made a solemn promise that all my life my main purpose would be to help other cerebral-palsied people in any and every way that I could. I told John about some of my castles in the air and he said, 'It sounds a crazy idea to me, but I believe you will do it. It is the crazy people that get on in this world.'

The road ahead was a difficult one. What I was learning in individual work had to be carried into everyday life. With skis I could walk anywhere, but I did not like using them unless some able-bodied person was near at hand, as I was so afraid of falling. Emotionally I was still rather unstable and when being taught a new movement that was hard I often cried from sheer frustration. Or, if I could not get what I wanted, I screamed with rage and was promptly put in the bathroom to calm down. I was not an easy child to help because in three years of hospital life nobody had cared about what I did or how I did it. Until Mrs. Collis came I was in the habit of thinking, 'Why try, who cares?' but from that first Saturday morning Mrs. Collis had shown me that she cared about what I did, and, more important still, how I did it. She was the first person outside my family who really minded about me and because there was a very real love between us I gradually became more responsive and my temper lessened.

By now I could sit properly on a chair or on the floor; I could stand in a corner of the room; I could walk with skis and I was beginning to walk with the 'crab', but this was very hard work. It was so nice to go alone to the W.C., and it was good to wash myself without help. Sitting on the floor I could dress myself in about a quarter of an hour, except for doing up buttons and boot-laces. I had stopped dribbling, but any effort —even holding a pencil—was enough to make me lose control and start again. Now when I did something that I had not done before I used my right hand, and so of course I was using this hand more and more, although previously it had been practically useless. I still fed myself with the left hand, but now there was no mess and all the food went into my mouth instead of onto the floor. Speech was a lot better, too. I was on the road to improvement. It had not been easy, but some of it had been fun and I had learned to do many things. But, above all, I had learned to stand up for what I believed to be right. I was beginning to be an individual and not just another child in the ward. I began to wonder what the future would bring; would Mrs. Collis's work be recognized one day, and how far would I go on improving? It was impossible to answer these questions at this stage.

Sometimes Mrs. Collis would look at me for a long time and then say, 'If only you had been born fifteen years later, I could have helped you much more. You were born fifteen years too soon.'

I would answer, 'Well, I have been in and out of hospitals all my life and I think the doctors have done everything they can, except operate. One day, when I can write much better, I will write a book about everything that has happened.'

'You had better write your autobiography one day, Vera,' Mrs. Collis replied, 'but it would be wiser to wait until after the war and we can have a long talk about it then.'

All the children in the ward were improving in their ability to do things and as they became happier, more normal children, their general health improved too and it gradually became a rare thing for any of them to have to be kept in bed. We had our temperatures taken only when we were ill and certainly not every day.

There were all kinds of children in the ward—girls and boys, big ones, little ones, good and bad ones; and even black, red, and yellow ones and some blue babies! They were from all countries and of all creeds; the one thing they had in common was cerebral palsy. Some had a severe handicap and others a slight one. There was Adele, aged ten, who could say nothing and who made different signs with her hands or arms to indicate what she wanted. Then there was eight-years-old Paul who was very cheeky until one day I smacked him rather harder than was intended and almost knocked him out. Most of the children were really beautiful and seemed to have some angelic quality in their faces. It was difficult not to love them when they were relaxed and happy, but when they became tense and cross their faces and bodies were transformed into grotesque shapes as they lost control of their muscles. Of course, I was the same as the rest, but being older than they were I somehow imagined myself to be different.

The new ideas about cerebral palsy were beginning to be talked about far beyond the walls of the hospital, and Mrs. Collis was getting all sorts of visitors. Some of them were really interested in the work, others came merely out of curiosity. M.P.s and doctors, people from all over the world and of different colours, came to ask questions and pass comment. Sometimes I could not help singing to myself the Sunday school chorus 'Red and yellow, black and white, they are all blessed in His sight'.

I had always been very shy but now, whenever someone interesting came to visit Mrs. Collis, she would bring them to see me, saying, 'Come and meet Vera, she can tell you quite a lot about the work.'

Then she would ask me to show them how I did my work, especially how I had learned to 'let go' my self-imposed stiffness and I would get down on the floor and show them how to go floppy and rid myself of my supposed 'spasticity'. They asked many questions and gradually I became accustomed to talking to other people and so lost all my shyness.

Mrs. Collis was now responsible for the treatment of ten children. There was a growing volume of office work to do and this, combined with fire-watching duties, often kept her in the hospital until the early hours of the morning. It was obvious that if she did not have help soon she would have a nervous breakdown and so she made many visits to County Hall to get some extra staff whom she could train. It had been her idea for a long time to have a team of people working together within the hospital, but as a separate unit. She longed to get away from the idea that we were sick children.

Many doctors came from County Hall to see how we were progressing and they noticed that all the children who had been having treatment, especially Brian, were much better. Brian had improved so much under such difficult conditions that the authorities at last decided to give Mrs. Collis her own unit and her own team of workers, but before the unit came to life the war had its part to play in our story.

6

Brentwood

In June 1944 Hitler started sending over his V.2s and it was decided, once again, that Queen Mary's Hospital should be evacuated. Most of the children were sent to the north of England, but the twelve of us who were under Mrs. Collis's supervision went to a women's hospital at Brentwood.

Most of the patients at Brentwood were epileptics and suffered from fits. They occupied the main part of the hospital while we were given the use of a block consisting of two dormitories, a day-room, kitchen, bathrooms, etc. We were a self-contained unit with Mrs. Collis in charge and nurses under her.

The teacher we had had at Queen Mary's had gone north with the other children, so a new young lady, Miss Judy Hernshaw, came to teach us. She was only a few years older than myself and when we were alone I always called her by her Christian name. Mrs. Collis told Judy to treat us as nearly as possible as normal people and this she always tried to do. She put her whole heart into her work but not many people realized this. They thought that as she had so small a class she was getting 'money for jam'. They forgot that she not only had to teach us the usual things children learn in school, she also had to stop us from doing them in the way which came easiest to us and try to make us do them in the way a normal person would.

Judy soon discovered that I could read only a very few

words and, as she was so busy with the younger children, she made John my teacher. I was given a very simple book and was told to read him a page each day. John was a very hard taskmaster and never allowed me to be lazy. If he thought I was not working hard enough he would say, 'If you do not read better than that I will tell all the little children what a baby you are!'

If the younger ones had known how backward I was they would have teased me, and this was the last thing I wanted, so I always made great efforts; but somehow reading has never come very easily to me.

Everyone worked hard at school in the mornings and enjoyed it very much; we all liked being treated as normal human beings. Most of the children were not ready to use a pencil as, by grasping it, they tensed their muscles too much, so they had to do their sums by putting big wooden numbers in the place for the answers. English was done in much the same way. Of course this meant a lot of carpentry for Judy as she could not get ready-made wooden numbers and things like that during the war. Some of the more handicapped children were unable even to hold big pieces of wood and the teacher had to sit by them and write down the answers as they said them. In this way everybody did some work and most did quite a lot.

In the afternoons we painted. Judy bought some patty tins, such as are used for baking small cakes, and put different coloured paints in each hole. Then she gave each one of us a big jar of clean water and a large sheet of cheap drawing paper stuck to our tables with sticky paper. Every child had his own chair and table made to suit his requirements, as the cerebral-palsied child must have furniture that fits him, otherwise he cannot work or play properly. Judy then gave us big brushes with large wooden handles and we had fun trying to paint. She did not mind how much mess we made so long as we got a picture on the paper. At this time I was still very unsteady, so I often painted myself as well as the table and floor. Sometimes John, who sat beside me, would get blue or green spots on his face and quite often I finished by accidentally tipping the water over everything. I tried to paint all sorts of things, but I can always remember the first thing I attempted. It was supposed to be an oak tree in a field with a blue sky and little white clouds going by, but what it actually looked like was a brown smudge in the centre of a piece of paper covered with green paint. Gradually my pictures took on a definite shape and painting became one of my most enjoyable pastimes.

Soon after we arrived at Brentwood Mrs. Collis was given an assistant, named Mrs. Buck, who was a doctor, and while Mrs. Collis worked with the more difficult children Mrs. Buck helped people like Rita, John and myself. The room we had to work in was much bigger than the one at Queen Mary's, so of course it was easier for us as we were not afraid of knocking things over or of hurting ourselves. It was here that Miss Kember came to join us while she was still a student of Occupational Therapy. She had been a music teacher before she heard of Mrs. Collis, and this knowledge was invaluable. Both Miss Kember and Mrs. Buck were learning all they could, one to help her own daughter, who was handicapped, and the other because she liked the work.

During the day they each worked in different ways in the same room, which was not a very good idea as Mrs. Buck had to have silence for her work, while Miss Kember's job could be anything but quiet; but after tea they sat all the children on the treatment-room floor and played lotto with them until bedtime. I often wondered who enjoyed the game most—the children or the staff.

One day Mrs. Collis came into the schoolroom and astonished us all by saying, 'How would you like to give a concert? If you do it well enough a lot of people will come and hear it.' We eagerly agreed to do our best, so for half an hour each day we had band rehearsal. To beat a drum or knock a tambourine was difficult for most of us, but to do it at the right moment and to keep on doing it was very hard work and needed a lot of concentration. However, we loved it and practised the same tunes so much that I often dreamt about them. Mrs. Collis realized that when in front of a big audience cerebral-palsied children would probably become nervous and shy, like normal children, but with worse results. For this reason she asked the matron to send about a dozen patients to the ward every day to get us used to being watched. All the women sat against the dark wall behind us and there was always a nurse with them ready to drag them out by the legs if any of them had a fit. These women were not classed as being mentally deficient, but some of them were not very intelligent, and as they sat there they made odd remarks such as, 'Ain't it a shame that they can't walk,' 'Poor little things,' 'Aren't they lovely and sweet,' etc. If anyone hit the drum at the wrong time they would say, 'Ain't he clever?' One of the women said to Mrs. Collis one day, 'Have you got a lot of foreign children here, because I can't understand them?' This was a standing joke amongst us for a long time.

It was a dry and sunny autumn that year and we spent most of our spare time in the orchard outside the ward. After the first few weeks the resident patients must have thought the children looked bored, because they would come and put the younger ones in wheel-chairs and take them out for walks. Our nurses were always busy and often they did not notice anything had happened until they came to look for the children and found them gone. Then we all had to go out and look for them, John pushing me in a wheel-chair, and when we found them the women would say, 'We thought the poor little things would like to go for a walk.'

One cloudy Saturday afternoon John and I went to the shed at the bottom of our ward. Half of it was used to keep the hospital fair equipment in and for storing emergency fire-fighting equipment, and the other half was empty. There was a wall to separate the two halves and we went into the empty half to get out of the wind. While we were there we heard a noise like someone trying to knit; it was the click, click of the needles that made us stop talking and listen.

'John,' I said, 'do you hear what I hear?'

'I think so, Vera; I wonder where it is coming from?'

'I think it is coming from next door.'

'But, Vera, nobody can get in there, that big barrow is in the way. Of course it might be haunted. Stop here and I will have a look round the front.'

When John came back he said he could see nobody but after a lot of searching we found a very small hole in the wooden partition and John put his eye to it. He could see a human leg and a ball of pink wool, and it turned out to be one of the women who used to sit and knit all day long on a coil of fireman's hose at the back of the fair shed. We never found out how she got in there or why she did it, but she gave us a fright that day and we did not go in there again.

Sometimes John and I were invited to a film show in the main hospital and it was amazing to see how the audience gradually disappeared during a performance. There were always nurses ready to take out any of the patients who felt ill. The same thing happened when we went to the hospital church to the Harvest Thanksgiving Service, and it was in this lovely church that John and I took our first Communion.

The church was packed with women and nurses, and the nurse at the door told us to sit in the front row so that the vicar would not have far to bring the bread and wine. We sat like two stuffed dummies, not daring to move because everyone could see us, but we enjoyed the service and then watched everyone go up to the communion rail. At last our turn came. The vicar gave me mine first and everything was all right. Then he tried to give John the bread, but John just could not open his mouth. The more he tried to open it the tighter it shut. The vicar kept saying, 'Don't you want this bread, it is very nice, do open your mouth, I have not got all day.' The old man got very cross, John began to cry and tears ran down his cheeks. I could feel every eye in that church looking at us and it was awful. I wanted to shout out, 'He can't help it.' I never felt so small in all my life. After about three minutes that seemed like eternity I said to John as quietly as I could, 'Don't worry, John, think about something else,' and I kept talking to him and this did the trick. After that awful day John said, 'I will never take Communion in a church again.' I often wonder if he did.

After tea in late September, while the nurses were putting the children to bed, we two used to go into the orchard and sit under the apple trees. The main road ran along the bottom and we could sit and watch the traffic go by while we waited for the rosy round apples to fall into our laps or drop on to our heads. Sometimes we talked and at other times John would sing to me. He had a very nice small voice and when nobody was about he would sing and sing. His favourite tune at that time was 'Lily Marlene' and its familiar melody always takes me back in memory to those sunny days under the apple trees. It sounded so lovely in the open air with the blue sky above and the sun just going down and life seemed good. I will long remember those evenings and the lovely times we had.

One day John and I found ourselves in a part of the hospital where we had not been before and we came across a lot of weary-looking apple trees in what looked like the hospital coal-yard. I said to John, 'I wonder what went wrong with them, the apples look all right.'

'I will leave you here for a minute while I go and investigate the trees,' said John, and he went behind one of the heaps of coal and out of sight. While he was gone one of the strange old women appeared and came up to me saying, 'What are you doing here, dear? Shall I take you for a nice walk?'

'No, thank you, I'm waiting for my friend.'

'I will go and ask him if I can take you to see the pretty flowers.'

'You'd better not do that, my friend can't speak,' I said in a scared voice. Before she could say any more John returned and ran all the way home, pushing me in the chair. (I could get around now by pushing something in front of me, but I still could not walk very far.) We were always a bit afraid of some of the women patients as it was impossible to know what they would do next. Besides that, they did not like having baths and our noses always told us that they were around even if we could not see them. We knew that they could not help doing the things they did, so we tried to keep out of their way.

We had a great deal of freedom at Brentwood and were allowed to go out whenever we chose. Mum often came down on a weekday and took John and me to the cinema in the town. I can remember how I enjoyed my first technicolor film. Rita Hayworth was the star and she danced and sang 'Long Ago and Far Away'. How I longed to be able to dance like that! I could feel my feet wanting to dance under my seat and I wanted to do high kicks all round the building. Although we enjoyed ourselves at the pictures, we enjoyed much more the week-ends when Mum and Gladys took us through the town, past the pond where little boys sailed their boats or caught tiddlers, and on to the common and beyond.

Nothing is more cherished than the memories of those Sunday afternoons. The tall bracken wore its autumn dress of red and green; the oak trees were just turning brown and all the country-side became indescribably colourful. There was a thick green carpet to walk on and a truly English blue sky. We would go for very long walks across that beautiful open place and Mum, Gladys and John (Gladys pushing me) would go on walking for hours, enjoying every minute of it. Even now when I think of that common I can feel the light, cool wind on my cheek. Everyday life seemed far away; the hospital with its unnatural pattern of living; the war with all its horrors; even the town with its small shops and big cinemas. Surely going across that common we were very near heaven? We would only start for home when the church bells called people to evensong and the sun was sinking in the west.

On Monday mornings I often tried to tell Mrs. Collis what a lovely time we had had at the week-end, but because we both had our own work to do we could not have a good talk. So one day, after tea, she took me to her room in the nurses' home where we had a long talk and then for a while I listened to her small radio. This was a great treat as there were no radios in the hospital wards. Unfortunately Mrs. Collis got into trouble the next day for taking me to her room; without knowing it she had broken a hospital rule. The next time she wanted to give me a night out she had to take me for a walk.

We had been evacuated to Brentwood to get away from the war and the bombing, but in actual fact we ran more into the danger zone. Anyway, the hospital was not a suitable place for us, as the young children were often afraid of the old women, and nobody could stop the women coming to visit the 'dear little babies'. After about four or five months, at Mrs. Collis's request, we went back to Queen Mary's Hospital and a new kind of life. Looking back I often smile about the time we spent at Brentwood and the people who were there with me also think of it with a twinkle in their eyes.

On arrival at Queen Mary's we were taken to a ward at the farthest point of the hospital. It was approximately two and a half miles from the gate and had previously been used as a nurses' training school. We had the use of the whole block consisting of two dormitories, two day-rooms, two kitchens, etc. There were still only twelve children in our little group, so one of the dormitories was converted into a school-room and one of the day-rooms became a dining-room, while the other was used as a room for activities. The rest of the hospital was completely deserted; all the other children were still evacuated and so we had a great deal of freedom, unhampered by the usual hospital restrictions.

Though we were actually living in a hospital, Mrs Collis wanted to get away from the idea that children with cerebral palsy are sick. That is why she called the whole block the Cerebral Palsy Unit, and it has been called that ever since. To make sure that we were treated as healthy children, the nurses who had been with us at Brentwood were sent up north to look after the sick children and four orderlies were employed to care for us.

E

Soon it was Christmas once again, but because of the war and the fact that the hospital was almost empty, the festive season passed very quietly. However, we all enjoyed ourselves and shortly afterwards Mrs. Collis allowed John and me to go home for a week's holiday. Mother was then living in a three-roomed flat over some shops in the city of London. Because of the stairs and the bitter weather I was unable to go out much, and all I can remember of that holiday is that I did not want to go back to the unit. It was the first time I had been home in years and I enjoyed being the centre of attraction for a while. Besides this, my Aunt Queen lived near by and I was able to get to know her and her family, who had previously been strangers to me. They had lived in Hull at the time when I first went into hospital, and in my fertile imagination Aunt Queen had always been a queen wearing a crown, and the place she lived in was 'Hell'! It came as rather a surprise to find that she was an ordinary human being with a very warm heart.

The week at home passed all too quickly and soon I was back on the unit. To make matters worse John was still away. I cried and cried, and when Mrs. Collis asked what was wrong, I sobbed, 'Let me go home, I want to go home.' To this she sternly replied, 'You will go home when I let you.' The next day John returned and after we had had a good cry on each other's shoulders we felt much better.

A week after our holiday the day of the concert arrived. The concert—the event for which we had been working and waiting for such a long time. I woke that morning and saw my dress over a chair, all nicely ironed and ready for the afternoon. As I looked at it a butterfly awoke in my stomach, so to deaden it I got up and dressed. After breakfast we all helped to put the finishing touches to the stage (five big tables lashed together) in the schoolroom. There was a red, white and blue cloth right across the front with some green leaves in vases on the floor. (We could not get any flowers as it was January.) Then, after the final rehearsal, we had our dinner.

The excitement rose as I sat before the mirror changing

from a drab navy-blue drill-slip and jumper into my dream dress. It was made of white organdie scattered with little forget-me-nots. Two little blue bows of ribbon sat on the shoulders, and the skirt, yards and yards of it, billowed around me like a cloud. I kept my black boots on and knew they would not show. Then Miss Kember and Judy covered my face with theatrical make-up and fixed a big white rose in my hair.

The schoolroom was full of chairs for our audience so to get on to the 'stage' I had to be taken out through a side door and brought back through the front door. Out into the snow wearing only a very thin dance dress it was chilly and Miss Kember worried that I would catch cold, but excitement kept me warm. At last I was on the stage with the others and looked down at the room packed with people. Brian had his drum tied to the arm of his chair so that he could bang it carefully. All the children looked very smart sitting there, the little girls in clean jumpers and drill-slips and the boys in grey suits. Mrs. Collis, looking handsome in a black dress, stood up to say a few words of introduction and I felt very proud of her.

The show was on. We all played together, then John and Betty danced their version of the polka—very well, but rather like two puppets with unseen hands pulling the strings. Sylvia and Lily, two shaky little girls, sang a song. We all did something on our own or in small groups and the audience loved it. Quite near the end it was my turn. Judy came on to the stage to help me from the chair to the floor, and while Miss Kember picked up her 'cello I knelt holding the skirt of my dress. I must have looked like a great big tea-cosy! To the music of the 'cello and piano I danced; my knees never left the floor but my arms circled the air and my body swayed to and fro, rhythmically, in time to the music, while I tried hard to achieve the poise and grace of a ballerina. When the dance ended everyone applauded and I felt exhilarated.

The last item of our show was given by Rita, who sang 'Twinkle, twinkle, little star', or rather 'Wikal, wikal, li'al tar'. She was standing in front of me, singing in her pretty little way, when she began to wobble this way and that. Perhaps it was wrong but I wanted to laugh, she looked so funny. Then she began to fall backwards—'Tighten your buttocks, Rita,' I murmured, prodding gently at her seat as she toppled towards me. This steadied her but it was a relief for everyone when she had finished. We ended that wonderful day with a gay party, partly to celebrate our success and partly because it was also my seventeenth birthday.

Now that Mrs. Collis had her own unit she was able to use, with effect, new ways of helping us, and she obtained better equipment for the schoolroom. Some of the results of her intensive study helped us and some had to be discarded as useless. She was developing a new attitude to the disability of which I am one of the victims. Often I lay naked on the table for an hour or two so that she could learn more and more about the nature of my movements. In fact I became a human guinea-pig and she used to say she knew more about my way of moving than about her own. All the time I went on improving—very slowly, but I was improving.

In the schoolroom each child had his own table and chair with his name painted in large letters across the back; there were also individual tables and chairs in the dining-room for those children who could not feed themselves, while the rest of us sat at a long table. I sat at the head in order to keep an eye on everyone. Quite a number of the younger or more badly handicapped children had to be washed and dressed and carried into the dining-room, so those who were first at the table often had a long wait before getting their meals. Naturally it was difficult for them to sit quietly during this wait and I made a point of going into the dining-room first to tell them stories or play games like 'I spy' or 'I went shopping'.

Very often one of the children would say, 'Tease, Adele, please, Vera, tease her.'

'Why should I tease poor Adele?' I would ask, laughing.

'Because we like to hear that funny noise she makes.' When Adele became annoyed she made a noise rather like someone singing up and down a scale, very much out of tune; this was the only noise she could make; she was unable to talk at all.

'You naughty children, shall I tease *you*?' I would answer.

Adele would give me a knowing look, and the next two or three minutes would be chaos as I pretended to tease her. It always ended with everyone having a good laugh. Adele was a good actress and I believe she used to like being teased.

By now I was helping Judy in the schoolroom and was enjoying life to the full. The best time of the day was suppertime. By seven o'clock all the youngsters were in bed and John and I had our supper in the quiet, empty dining-room. It was then that we really got to know each other and he would tell me about his childhood. He knew my Aunt Queen as well as I knew his Uncle Bill and I often told him about my hopes and fears for the future. We would sit by the window watching the sun go down, or else sit by the fire and roast chestnuts. When they were ready John would knock them out with a poker and they were delicious.

At about 8 o'clock we were bathed and put to bed where we could read until lights out at 10 p.m. One night as I walked with my crab past Mrs. Collis's office she was still at work and she called out, 'Vera, can you bathe yourself?'

'Not yet,' I replied.

'Call me when you are undressed.'

It took me about ten minutes, sitting on the floor, to take off my clothes, then Mrs. Collis came into the bathroom.

'How do you get into the bath?' she asked.

'Somebody puts me in.'

Mrs. Collis told me how to get into the bath without help and how to bathe myself. It was a wonderful feeling to be independent in so personal a matter as taking a bath, and after a little practice I never needed an orderly to help again.

About six months after we had returned to Queen Mary's the war in Europe came to an end. Mrs. Watson, one of our married orderlies, lived just outside the hospital and she asked permission to take John to the party which she and a few other women were giving for the children living in their street. Unfortunately for her John went home for a holiday at that time and so she had to take me—a very poor substitute.

We were given a very nice tea and then I watched as the children played games and had fun, and I experienced a strange sensation. For so long I had been living with handicapped children that seeing normal children play and do the things which I knew I could never do made me want to cry—somehow it did not seem right.

The games lasted for about an hour and then Mrs. Watson took me into her house for a while before going back to the unit. As we entered her front room I saw my dear old friend, my tricycle—only it was no longer mine because Mum had sold it to Mrs. Watson for her little son. In any case it was no longer of any use to me as I had outgrown it, but seeing it once again brought back a tide of happy memories and I longed to throw my arms around the handle-bars and kiss them. Thoughts sped back to the days when Dad had been alive and this bicycle had been my key to freedom. Lovely days cycling over the common; days before I realized that I was 'different' from other children. Quickly my mind raced forward through all the changes that had taken place in the years between. What did the future hold for me? Now that I was seventeen surely even the determined Mrs. Collis would be unable to keep me at the unit much longer. I should have been discharged a year ago, either to go home or to become a patient in a women's hospital for the chronic sick. It would have been nice to go home, but I knew in that way I would never get any better and it would have been hard work for Mum to carry me up and down the stairs to the flat. I dared not think of the alternative—to be a patient in a ward for the chronic sick seemed like being condemned to a life sentence in prison for a crime I had not committed.

7

School

By early summer 1945 Queen Mary's Hospital was back in full swing with children in many of the wards. Nothing more had been said about my discharge, but as space was limited, and there was a long waiting list for the unit, I was transferred, for a time, to a ward. I believed I was being sent away because it was thought I would not improve much more. I had progressed well enough to stand alone for a few seconds, to feed myself and attend to most of my toilet needs, but it was still very hard work to do my hair and things like that.

I left the unit with a broken heart. Although the ward I was transferred to was only next door to the unit I felt very lonely, very lonely indeed. All my friends were in the unit and I could not have felt lonelier if I had been sent to China.

In the ward I could do practically nothing; I could not knit and sewing had been banned because when trying to grasp so small a thing as a needle my tendency was to tighten my whole body and lose control of my handicap. There was nothing for it but to read and read and read. My crab, being part of the equipment of the unit, remained there, and without it I felt helpless.

All the other children who from time to time and for various reasons had left the unit had either gone home or been sent to wards where they received physiotherapy as before. This meant that Mrs. Collis did not see them again and this was the fate that I believed was in store for me.

For a few weeks I was utterly miserable and then one wonderful day Mrs. Collis came to the ward and told me that she had managed to arrange for me to go back to the unit for short periods daily. At first I went only for individual work, but later on it was to help in the schoolroom as well, and no one could realize how much I looked forward to this work, for here, instead of being a helpless nuisance, I could really be useful and help others.

It is true lessons were given in the ward, but I could not help the teacher there in the same way as I helped Judy because not many of the children had cerebral palsy. They had all sorts of other handicaps. Some were pathetically deformed and others had only a short time to live; some were mentally deficient or had water on the brain. There were two little boys who were incontinent because there was something wrong with the base of their spine, and one of them also had a weak foot. There was nothing else wrong with them, but they had been in hospital since birth and were naturally a little behind other children in experience. Every Sunday at visiting time these two little boys walked to the front door to wait for their mothers. Every Sunday, summer or winter, wet or fine, they waited there in vain until the nurse called them for tea. Their mothers never came, nor did their fathers or any other relatives. Unfortunately this was not an isolated case; there were many children who could not walk but who kept their eyes fixed on the door for hours on end and looked longingly at all the other mothers who came to visit the other luckier children.

Whenever I saw a child whom I thought Mrs. Collis could help I would tell her about him and she would examine him to see if he would benefit by being transferred to the unit. By now I had become quite expert at diagnosing cerebral palsy and was able to help three or four children in this way.

There was nothing to do in the evenings in the ward so I used to go to bed early and read and soon I began to enjoy such books as *Little Women* and Dickens's novels. Adele had come to join me in the ward and she often longed to know what I was reading. I could not read aloud to her because I could not pronounce all the words correctly, so I used to read a chapter to myself and then retell it to her. She never knew how much of the story I made up when I could not remember the book, but she seemed to enjoy it all.

It is surprising how much one can learn about a person who cannot talk by simply asking them questions to which they need only shake or nod their head. I could not talk *with* Adele but I used to talk *to* her for hours. She loved it and was a very good listener.

Once a month Communion was given in the hospital wards. As John was now the only communicant in the unit he came to our ward for this service. In school the day before he would say, 'Be up early tomorrow, I will be over at about 6 o'clock,' and promptly at 6 a.m. I would be waiting for him in the sister's office. Usually he would bring with him a single flower, saying, 'This is for your button-hole, Vera, I picked it on the way over.'

The vicar started his rounds early as he had a number of wards to visit, but it was generally 7 a.m. before he reached us because he always left us till last. He knew how friendly John and I were and that hour, once a month, was now the only time we could be together alone.

During the summer Mum and Gladys regularly visited me on alternate Sunday afternoons, but on the week-end when they did not come I was rather at a loss to know what to do. One day I had an idea, I would go to see John every other Sunday and perhaps on Saturdays, too. I would not be missed on the ward during visiting time and I could get back in time for tea. In order to meet John I had to leave my wheel-chair at the edge of the grass slope at the back of the ward and crawl towards the old brown hut that stood at the back of the unit. When almost there I would sing—or try to—the first line of 'Drink to me Only' and then after a few seconds John's head would pop out of the hut singing the second line. In the centre of the field behind the unit was a piece of ground that had once been a garden but had become overgrown by weeds, and in the middle of the weeds was a manhole cover that made a kind of seat. John always covered this with a red blanket and, while munching sweets saved from our mother's ration, we would talk and talk for about an hour. Then I would crawl back to the ward, sometimes cutting my knees on the way.

All too soon winter came and a very quiet Christmas, after which most of the children on the unit caught 'flu and I was unable to go to school. Life became very uninteresting. I could not even comfort myself by painting, as the ward teacher thought it a waste to give me a large sheet of paper and I was quite unable to paint on a small sheet. Adele was the only person in the ward near my own age and I spent most of the time either talking to her or trying to help her to talk to me by passing on some of the tips Miss Wood had given me in speech therapy. The only bright spots during this time were when the therapists from the unit came over to see me. I will never forget the day Miss Kember gaily announced that my propelling chair had arrived. I was very excited as I longed to have a chair that I could drive myself when I went home and of course I imagined it would be a motor chair. Imagine my disappointment when it turned out to be an ordinary wheel-chair. My heart sank into my boots because I knew I could not get far in that, but I pretended to be pleased as I did not want to seem ungrateful.

Then one day I caught a very bad cold and had to stay in bed for a week and while there Mrs. Collis came visiting twice and cheered me up a great deal. The following Monday I went back to the unit for lessons and as the hands of the clock turned towards noon one of the orderlies came to me and said, 'Take your crab and go into the dining-room.'

'But, Anne,' I protested, 'I go back for dinner.'

'I was told to tell you to go into the other room,' she insisted.

Willingly I obeyed. During the meal Mrs. Collis walked in, stood by the fire, looked at me for a minute and said, 'You are not going back to the ward. I think you can be useful to us if you live here again—or would you like to go back?'

School

My eyes must have told her the answer because she went on, 'Come to my office at 2 o'clock, I want to talk to you.'

At 1.45, with the aid of the crab, I went out of the school-room, across the courtyard, through the dormitory and was at her office by 2 o'clock. The distance was not much more than 100 yards, but even with the aid of the crab I could walk only very slowly. I went into her office and sat in the armchair.

'Are you pleased to be back, Vera?'

'Oh, yes, I feel as if I have come home.'

'You have not come back as a child; I want to give you a job. Besides helping in the schoolroom you will sit in the dormitory after dinner and keep the small children quiet while they have a rest, and I will give you other jobs from time to time.'

I was delighted at the news and said so at supper that night. John was so pleased that he proposed a toast and drank my health—in milk!

At this time Mother had just suffered another bereavement. Her father, a grand old man who had always been most active, died at the ripe old age of ninety-five. Everyone loved him and although we knew he could not live for ever we were sorry that he had not lived to see his centenary. After visiting her old home for the funeral Mother brought back with her all the books she had received as prizes at school. They were slightly yellow with age but were in very good condition and contained some interesting stories. On visiting day she brought the books to me and they gave me an idea. It was my job when the order-lies had taken the children into school to keep them amused until the teacher came. It was not always easy to do this and keep the room tidy as well, so one day I asked, 'Would you like a story?'

Some said 'No' and others 'Yes', so I gave the babies some-thing to do and told the children who did not want to listen to play quietly. Sitting on a low chair I began to tell the story I had read in bed the night before. It was a sad story (they pre-ferred sad stories to happy ones) and soon the children who had been playing stopped and sat on the floor beside me, the room became very quiet and some of the children had tears in their eyes. I paused 'Don't you like the story, shall I stop?'

'Oh, no, Vera, what happens next? We love it.'

The room was very quiet when Judy came in and she wondered what had happened. The questions those children asked! Each night I read a chapter or two and each morning I told them all about it. They were quite disappointed when we came to the last book and there were no more stories to be read.

At 9.30 each morning school started with prayers around the piano. As soon as these were over all the children took their places at their desks while I handed out the boxes containing their books and pencils. I did this by putting all the boxes on a chair and then pushing it around in front of me. This task accomplished I took my place between Peter and Brian.

I sat with Peter and Brian not for a week or a month, not even for a term, but for years. I do not regret it and would do the same again if necessary. Peter was very wild in his movements and his uncontrollable arms and legs used to shoot out in all directions. When he was reading I had to stand behind him and help him to keep his head straight. I used to try to get him to keep his hands in his lap, but even so he accidentally gave me several black eyes. When he shot an arm up into the air I would grasp it firmly and ask him to think of what he was doing, then guide it gently back into his lap. Both the boys had difficulty in speaking, but Peter was partly deaf as well.

Peter shouted when he spoke but Brian spoke on the inward breath. Peter had lived at home until he came to the unit, but Brian had lived in hospital all his life. In spite of this Brian was more advanced than Peter, who was two or three years his senior, and was of normal intelligence. Years before Brian had had an operation to uncross his legs and this made it unlikely that he would ever walk, so he concentrated on improving the use of his arms.

Brian could not control his facial muscles and sometimes produced hideous expressions. On visiting day I often told

Mum about him and she would say, 'Don't play with him. He is silly, you can see by his face. Why don't you play with that little girl over there, there is not much wrong with her.'

I could not make her understand that the girl with less handicap was rather silly while Brian was of above average intelligence. Some children with cerebral palsy are mentally deficient whereas others are perfectly normal—the degree of their handicap has no bearing on their intelligence, this depends entirely on the *part* of their brain which is damaged. Both Peter and Brian had defects but the damage produced entirely different results in each child. Peter was very unsteady and unpredictable in his movements, while Brian was tense and stiff and resisted any movement. Normally Brian would have been unsteady like Peter, but being of a higher intelligence he tried harder and stiffened to such an extent that he found it practically impossible to move at all. He could just give me his school box by dragging it across the table with his arm held stiff and straight.

Neither of the boys could hold a pencil or turn the pages of a book, and that was where I could be useful. The idea was that in teaching other children I would teach myself. Every morning I would say, 'Which lesson is first today, reading or sums?'

We did one before break and the other afterwards. When the boys did arithmetic Judy would write out a page of sums, from the example book, for each of them. I would show them how to do the sums and write down the answers as they worked them out, being careful not to do the actual working for them. Brian was about eight years old when I started helping him, he could count up to ten and was just beginning to read. Peter was not much more advanced so we started from the beginning. At first I used counters—not ordinary counters but anything from the children themselves to a box of pencils, or from the chairs to a box of bricks. This was to show them that people are counted in the same way as objects. Soon they progressed past the need for counters and most of their work was done from books.

Teaching the children to read was not done by starting with

the alphabet but by reading with them a book in which the same words were used so often they became imprinted upon their minds. The books used told a very simple story—one was about Old Lob, a farmer, and another about a cat and a ball. I read these books so often with Brian and Peter that I used to dream about them at night. In order to teach the boys and keep their respect I had always to be one leap ahead of them. Judy helped with this. On the whole they were good hard-working boys, but sometimes Brian used to think that I would do all the work. When he was in one of these lazy moods I used to reprimand him and then take away his school books and give him a box of bricks to play with while I helped someone else. This punishment proved more effective than any other; if Brian was put in a corner he would only turn round and make the other children laugh by making faces at them. The punishment meted out to him had to be something I could enforce myself. If it had been given by the teacher the children would have had no respect for me when the teacher was not in the room.

Judy noticed how much I enjoyed this work and said one day, 'Why do you take a book to bed, Vera? Is it to make sure the children never catch you out? Never let them do that if you can help it!'

When Brian could read well enough we often tackled books together and if there was a new word which we did not recognize he might say it was one thing and I another. To settle the argument we would ask John—never Judy—and sometimes Brian was right and I was wrong, much to my shame.

Half-way through the morning the children had a break for a quarter of an hour while they were given a drink and taken to the toilet. During this time I sat outside in the courtyard. The view from here was perfect. To the front and down each side were gently undulating fields bordered on one side by a dark green copse and on the other by a smallholding, where, when it was very quiet, we could hear the pigs squealing. A few private houses lay scattered along the hillside, too far away for us to see their occupants. It was lovely to sit here in the summer and when it was warm enough the children had their lessons in the open air, but the time when it was most picturesque was in winter when everything was covered with snow and there was not a blade of grass to be seen. It was during these mid-morning breaks that I thanked God for the beauty of the earth and gained strength of mind and body with which to tackle the rest of the day's work.

Sometimes Judy would say, 'Let Brian and Peter look after themselves today, I want you to hear the younger children so that I can take a lesson with the older ones.'

Then, as the little ones worked out their sums and put their wooden numbers in place, I wrote down the answers for them in a book and told them whether they were right or wrong.

There was one little boy, Alan, who had been a normal baby but who had had whooping cough at six months old and this had left him with cerebral palsy. For six years he had lain in a hospital cot and was fed on a bottle, with the result that he looked just like a large stiff baby when Mrs. Collis first brought him to the unit. The boy was fairly intelligent, but because he had always been treated as a baby he had the sense of a baby. With the right kind of handling he gradually grew up. Alan was about nine before he started to read. Judy and I used to try to make him read about Old Lob and all the animals but Alan just could not understand that the marks on the paper meant words. One day I was sitting by him, still trying but not hoping too much, when I was very surprised to hear him reading. I could not believe my ears. I called Judy and she said softly, 'I always knew he would read.' But the look in her eyes told how happy she was because we had both been wondering whether he would ever manage it. Judy used to make sure that she gave every child the education best suited to his mental development and most of the children learned to read quite easily, but it was always a day of rejoicing when someone like Alan reached that point.

One morning, when we were all working quietly, Judy asked me to get her a ruler.

'I can't, they are on the top shelf.'

'Well, stand on a chair then.'

'I'm sorry, I have a handicap and cannot stand on a chair,' I answered, smiling.

An embarrassed Judy turned round, 'I'm sorry, of course you can't. You see, Vera, I never think of you as being handicapped, as you do the job of a normal person.'

To my surprise and delight she meant every word she said. It was true I was very happy helping her and the work I did was not difficult but was more a matter of plodding steadily on day after day. If Judy went out to a lecture she would say to everybody, 'Vera is in charge, help her,' and then to me, 'Keep them quiet and occupied. They all have plenty to do at the moment but if anyone finishes their work before I come back give them a toy to play with.'

Usually the children behaved as well for me as they did for Judy, but when anyone was naughty I didn't say anything to them but just sat them in the corner to cool off. It surprised people to see how hard everyone worked with no teacher in the room, and as long as I was there they would be as good as gold; but if I went out and they were alone for a few minutes, there would be an uproar.

Things did not always go smoothly and I vividly remember one lovely summer day when I was in charge of a painting class working outside. A sudden cry made me look up to see Sylvia, a very pretty dark-haired child of eight, with her face covered in yellow paint; it was even in her mouth.

'Now what have you done?' I gasped. 'John, go and get an orderly for her, please.'

'Well, I always wanted to know what paint tasted like, now I know and I don't like it,' sobbed Sylvia.

'You look like a Chinaman. Don't touch anything and try not to swallow it as I don't want you to die.' Then I turned to the rest of the class and said, 'Stop laughing, it's not funny. Sylvia is a very silly girl.' I was worried that the child would poison herself. At that minute Judy and an orderly came out together and when Sylvia had gone in and Judy was clearing up the mess I apologized.

'I'm sorry, Judy. The last time I looked at Sylvia she was painting quite happily.'

'Don't worry, I expect this sort of thing to happen sometimes. I am glad she did not try it with black or white paint though, they are not very good for eating and that is why I don't use them much.'

Sylvia was given a mouth-wash and a dose of medicine and luckily was none the worse for her experience.

Sometimes Judy was called away from school before she had time to set anyone any work for the day. Then I would give the youngest children toys to play with and the older ones were given what we called 'sum puzzles'. These were two pieces of cardboard on one of which were put twelve sums— any kind of sum—and on the other piece were put the answers. A coloured picture was stuck to the reverse side of the second piece and then this was cut into twelve bits with an answer on each bit. When the child had put an answer on top of each sum he could turn the whole thing over, remove the top sheet of cardboard and if the answers were right of course the picture was right, too. The sum puzzles were a great favourite and kept the children quiet for ages, although of course sometimes they cheated and put the picture together first and then turned it over to look at the answers.

Often one of the children would look out of the window at the few far-away cottages and say, 'I wonder what it would be like to live in a house?' Then I used to put down my work and tell them about the outside world. About roads, buses and trains, about houses and how people lived in small rooms and not in dormitories and schoolrooms. It was hard for them to understand that when you buy food in shops you have to take it home and cook it before you eat it, as all hospital food came up from the kitchens ready for the table. It was very important to tell the children about everyday life so that when they went home to stay they would not feel too strange.

School

Judy often told us about her own childhood or about the wonderful things she had seen on the long walks she liked to take, and I saw the fruit of this kind of work on Saturdays. Then the children played all sorts of games and talked about everything. Their favourite game was mothers and fathers, with the mother going out shopping and buying some boiled potatoes and the father working at making meat.

Besides the children of school age we had about five other children between the ages of two and five. Sometimes it was my job to play with them. To be quite truthful I used to enjoy myself as much as the babies did. Children learn a great deal from watching their elders and then copying them so when the little ones were sitting at the water or sand tray I got busy building sand castles or playing with the water. Naturally I had to be very careful how I did this because the child might copy my mistakes. They knew I was different from the other people who looked after them and they tried hard to do things better than I could. Occasionally when a new child came to the unit he would be frightened by my shakiness and loud, gruff voice. To gain his confidence I would sit near him but play with another child. I did this to let him see that I was not an ogre. Sooner or later I would feel a small hand on my leg as I knelt at the next table. (I always knelt to play with the babies so as to be at the same height as them and not tower over them.) When the tiny hand touched my leg and I heard a small voice trying to say, 'Pick up my brick,' I felt as if something very warm had reached my heart. I was drunk with happiness because I had made a new friend and I cannot think of anything more sincere than the love of a child who sees that you can give him the help he needs.

One day the headmistress of the hospital school sent out a notice that there was to be a painting competition. We all entered for it. The subject was a vase of flowers and we did one picture each. Some of the pictures were of big flowers, some of little flowers, some were flowers of all one colour and others were of all the colours of the rainbow. Then we forgot all about the competition until one day we heard, to everyone's amazement, that we had won a prize. The children loved painting and they enjoyed going in for competitions. Being cerebral-palsied does not stop children from having a talent for painting, and many of their pictures were very colourful.

Shortly after this Judy made a tour of the hospital wards to compare the work of other patients with that of our children and she came back delighted. She discovered that not only were most of our children as far advanced as normal children, but in fact three of them, Brian, Sylvia and Lily, were forward for their age. This was presumably because, owing to their movement difficulties, all the children preferred to work at their lessons, which they could do well, rather than play at games which they could not do well.

8

I Become a Person

ᕙᕗ

At the time I was given a job in the unit I was also given a room of my own. It was what had been one of the 'separation' rooms and it was furnished with a bed, chair, table and chest of drawers. There was nothing grand about the furnishings, but to me it was heaven. To have a room of my very own, somewhere where I could shut the door and be completely alone— it was something I had dreamed of all the years I had slept in a dormitory and now it had come true. It was wonderful. The chest of drawers had one drawer which could be locked and here I put all my personal things and then hid the key.

On the mantelpiece stood two framed photographs, one of Dad and the other of Stanley. Whenever I was worried or troubled I shut myself in that little room and talked to these two photographs as if those two dear people were still alive. Maybe it was the solitude that helped, but somehow I felt I could hear Dad's voice telling me what to do, and following his advice I found my problems solved themselves.

When Stanley was killed all the crew of his plane died with him, including the pilot, Mick, who was an Australian. After the accident Gladys wrote to Mick's mother and this started a pen-friendship which has lasted to this day. During the days of rationing Mick's mother regularly sent us food parcels, and one of his sisters, who owned a sweetshop, often sent me big boxes of sweets. It was always a red letter day when one of these parcels arrived at the unit and after I had given about half the contents away the rest would be safely locked up in my drawer. It was surprising what a lady's life I could lead while this stock lasted. Money meant nothing to the children for there was nothing to buy in a children's hospital, but there were always plenty of willing helpers ready to wait on me hand and foot for the reward of a few sweets. Often in the morning a gentle tap would come on my door.

'Come in.' Sylvia would appear, pushing Lily in her wheel-chair. 'Hallo, what do you want?'

'We want to make your bed, Vera.'

'Have you made your own?'

'No, but we want to make yours because we love you.'

'All right, go ahead, and you can have some sweets but not till after tea,' I would say, laughing.

John also had a small room of his own and in the evening he often went to his room to read while I went to mine to paint. The hours seemed to fly past while I was busy with paint and paper, and it did not matter how much mess I made because now I could clear it up myself. One day I was really engrossed in painting a self-portrait and then, when it was almost completed, I accidentally dropped a big blob of black paint on the upper lip. It looked rather like a moustache. Disappointed, I left the picture on the table where it was found by Mrs. Collis who took it into the schoolroom to stick it on the wall.

'Did you do this, Vera?' she asked. 'It is very good. Who is it?'

I could not say it was me gone wrong, so thinking quickly, I replied, 'It is called "the artist" because he has long hair!'

That picture hung on the schoolroom wall for a long time and people must often have wondered why I laughed when I looked at it.

Time passed happily until January 1946 when Mrs. Collis was taken very ill with pneumonia. While she was away there was really no one to take her place. Miss Kember helped us with occupational therapy and one or two of the mothers of the children came in to do what they could. Mrs. Collis always welcomed the mothers of the children as voluntary workers on the unit. They used to watch her at work in the treatment room and then carry out her advice themselves so that they knew the best way to handle their children when they took them home.

Every day John and I went into the treatment room and tried to do our work alone. First we would lie on the floor and then go through our routine work of controlling our movement by thinking as we moved. We worked conscientiously in the beginning because we knew it was for our own good, but it was not easy with no one there to correct our faults and of course we could not learn anything new. We often asked Miss Kember or Judy how Mrs. Collis was, and they answered us truthfully, saying, 'She is still very ill,' or, 'She is a little better. I hope her strength keeps up.'

However, when we asked when she would be coming back, that was another story. No one knew.

Perhaps not so much to the younger children, but to John and me Mrs. Collis was much more than a researcher and a therapist, she was (and still is to me) a very good friend. John and I based our very lives on her; she not only helped our physical handicap, she helped us to be real people. When I was small I always tried to be good, mainly because I was afraid to be naughty. Like anyone else I could think for myself but I never expressed my thoughts, partly because of my speech difficulty and partly because I feared I would be ridiculed if my views were different from those of my elders. At home Gladys was my brain. If she liked something, I did, if she disliked someone, I did too. In hospital I always tried to be good and please everybody because I desperately wanted to be loved and admired.

Mrs. Collis often said to me, 'Don't be such a goody-goody. You are an individual. Let people know you have a mind of your own. Say what you think, not what they expect you to think. Try to grow up and express your own opinions. Have confidence in yourself and people will respect you for it.'

I used to see Mum for two hours every fortnight and that

was all, but Mrs. Collis was there every day and so I became very dependent on her and treated her like a mother. To John she was even more of a mother because his real mother lived so far away she was only able to visit him on bank holidays and during the summer holidays.

Days passed into weeks and weeks into months and still Mrs. Collis did not return. She was not only ill with pneumonia, she was also very tired and run down, and this delayed her recovery. By April she was still away and we all began to wonder whether she would ever get better. We tried to keep our feelings to ourselves but one day John came to me in a very troubled way and blurted out, 'Mrs. Collis has been away a very long time and I don't think she is ever coming back. What is going to happen to the unit now? I need not worry, my mother will always look after me, but I think it is a waste of time to go on doing this same old work every day.'

'Don't be silly, John,' I remonstrated, 'of course she will come back. Her work is not finished yet and it is our duty to carry out her instructions until she does return. Surely you want to go on improving as you did when she was here?'

It was no use. No matter what I said or did John would not believe that Mrs. Collis would come back. For three years he had worked very hard because a woman had loved him. She was the only one outside his family who had really loved and taken an interest in him, and now that she was no longer there he felt lonely and unwanted.

'Why should I bother to work hard, no one cares,' was his attitude. He still went through the movements of working each day, but his spirit was not in his work and he made no further progress. He just did not have any ambition left in life.

At night I lay in bed, thinking, thinking. There must be an answer somewhere. How could I make John believe that Mrs. Collis would come back? Would she come back, though? Doubts filled my mind. What would happen if she did not come back? My dear unit would be turned into a ward again, John would go home and I would never see him again, and

87

what would happen to me? I was eighteen and too old to stay in a children's hospital. It would be difficult for Mum to have me at home. The only alternative was the women's hospital for incurables. The very thought struck terror in my heart. 'For God's sake, not there,' I would cry into the darkness of the night. I would find myself in a cold sweat and when at last sleep did come my dreams were troubled by nightmares of what the future seemed to hold. My only comfort came from prayer and quietly I would turn to God and ask Him to send Mrs. Collis back to us and to stifle my fears of being put into an institution and left there until I died.

No matter what fear clutched my heart in the dark hours of the night, by day I tried to be calm. Judy and I knew that a lot depended on us. If the younger children sensed our despair they would no longer take any interest in their work and so, for their sakes, we kept up an appearance of cheerfulness.

One day Judy called to me, 'Miss Kember wants to work with you this afternoon. I have been to see Mrs. Collis and she says she hopes to be back soon. She asked me to tell you to keep working and help Miss Kember all you can.'

Mrs. Collis often sent us little messages such as this and so, although I was glad to know that she had our welfare at heart even while she was sick, I was not reassured that she would be returning to the unit. However, I went to see Miss Kember and, after we had gone through the routine work, she surprised me by saying, 'Wouldn't it be nice if you could walk by the time Mrs. Collis returns!'

'Oh, yes,' I agreed without enthusiasm, because I never really thought I would be able to walk even with Mrs. Collis's help and I was quite sure I wouldn't be able to do so without it. 'Shall we try? We will come in here every afternoon and practise walking,' Miss Kember replied, undaunted, and with a beautiful smile all over her kind face.

Now Miss Kember is a very tiny woman, 5 ft. 1 in., the same height as myself, and during these afternoon walking sessions she would stand behind me with her hands on my hips and say,

'Walk.' We must have looked like some queer double act from the music-hall stage, as we wended our way unsteadily up and down that treatment-room floor! All Miss Kember could see was the back of my head and on one occasion I lost my balance and fell over backwards. Of course I had a nice soft cushion to fall on as I landed on her tummy, but poor Miss Kember was not so lucky! Fortunately she did not hurt herself but I will always remember her sitting on the floor in the middle of the treatment-room, just laughing, and laughing, until she had a pain.

What Miss Kember did not know in those far-off days was that you do not teach a child to walk, or dress or feed himself in one combined effort. A baby goes through several stages before it is ready to walk—first it sits, then it crawls, later it stands and finally it walks. So it is with the cerebral-palsied child, but with an added difficulty. Quite apart from the damage to the brain, which makes movement difficult, there is also a pattern on the child's brain—caused by years of incorrect movement—which must be erased before the correct pattern can become imprinted there. It is obvious that the earlier a cerebral-palsied child receives treatment the more likely he is to benefit from it. I was fifteen before I received any correct treatment, therefore I had fifteen years of bad movement and posture habits to overcome before I could learn to do anything properly. Mrs. Collis had helped me a great deal towards this end and under her guidance I had gone through the stages of sitting, crawling, and standing, but I was not ready for walking just yet, and unknowingly I was deriving more harm than good from well-meant efforts to help.

Miss Kember was very much overworked in those days. Apart from what was still called 'occupational therapy'—that is, feeding, dressing and day-to-day activities of that kind, she had all the correspondence of the unit to deal with. One of the mothers used to give her a hand with this and one afternoon, after a particularly strenuous day, they both dropped exhausted into armchairs and put their feet up on the table.

'There's just time for a cigarette and ten minutes' rest before we go home,' said Miss Kember, when suddenly the door opened and the medical superintendent walked in. He stood there for a moment, apparently unable to believe his eyes, and then, in a very scathing tone, asked, 'Relaxing?!!'

One beautiful morning in May I woke to realize that summer had almost arrived. The birds were singing, the sun was high in the sky and outside the trees were resplendent in their brilliant green foliage. I went to work in a more peaceful frame of mind than for many a long day, and standing in front of the treatment mirror I casually noticed the reflection of three women coming along the front path. The short one was Miss Kember, the younger one was Judy, but who was the third? The figure was familiar—surely it couldn't be—yes, it was, it was Mrs. Collis. I was not dreaming, it was true, she had come back at last. Mixed feelings of joy, relief and thankfulness rushed through me, but suddenly I came back to earth with a bump. There was a terrible din in the schoolroom. What were those children up to? It sounded like a bear garden. 'Mrs. Collis must not come back to find the children misbehaving,' I thought, as pushing the crab in front of me I hurried out into the corridor. Pausing outside the schoolroom door, I called out to an orderly, 'What's for dinner today?' Then, in a much quieter tone, 'It's all right, I don't really want to know what's for dinner; it's just to give the children time to calm down before I go in.'

We both grinned and listened. Brian's low growling voice was heard, 'Vera's coming, be quiet.'

And then everyone joined in with, 'Sit down, Vera is coming.'

This was followed by a last desperate plea from Lily, 'Please, Barbara, sit down or Vera will tell you off.'

'Anyone would think I was the Devil himself,' I laughed.

The room was silent and the children sat at their desks doing their best to look like little angels. 'Good morning, everyone, you must all be very good today. Mrs. Collis is back and if you don't behave yourselves she will go away and never come back again,' I called out, unable to hold back the good news any longer.

'We don't believe you,' came the reply. 'You're only saying that so that we shan't be naughty.'

'If you don't believe me ask Mrs. Van when she comes in,' I retaliated. Judy had recently married a Dutchman and 'Mrs. Van' was short for her new lengthy married name which we found almost unpronounceable.

Mrs. Collis did not come into the schoolroom to see the children—in fact she was still far from well and it was some time before she started working with us regularly again. All her time was taken up in the office dealing with the mountains of correspondence that had piled up during her absence and which kept arriving by every post. Still, the fact that she was there was enough to put the children on their best behaviour and for the next few days they were very good indeed. Of course, like all small children, they were full of high spirits and by the week-end they were their usual noisy, mischievous selves once again, but they did realize that Mrs. Collis needed quiet during the hours she spent in her office so they usually waited until she had gone home before they started raising a riot!

Miss Kember continued helping us with day-to-day activities, Judy with our lessons, and Miss Wood helping us with speech. Mrs. Collis did all the clerical work and the orderlies did the housework and served the meals. There were no nurses at the unit and we were all very happy, but very little progress was being made. It is true the children's brains were being kept fully occupied with their lessons and other occupations, but their bodies were not getting the attention they needed because there was no one there to work with them scientifically. John and I were the exception to this rule. Mrs. Collis saw that while she had been away we had made no progress, in fact we had even regressed a little, so she spent all the time with us that she could spare. This was about an hour or so each week. Not much, but enough to show us our mistakes, and under her guidance I gradually improved until I reached the stage where I was ready to walk. Unfortunately John did not make the same headway. He had lost confidence in himself and no amount of reassurance could convince him that although he would never be normal he could lead a useful life. He was very homesick and only lived for the day when he could go home permanently.

Five months after Mrs. Collis had returned to the unit she called me into her office and casually remarked, 'I've written a book.'

'You've done what?' I gasped, unable to believe my ears. I had never known anyone who had written a book before and thought that anyone capable of doing so must be someone really marvellous.

Mrs. Collis calmly continued, 'I've written a book about cerebral palsy and you're one of the people I've dedicated it to. The book is called *A Way of Life for the Handicapped Child*.'

'Well, I hope it makes people realize that we can and should be helped,' I beamed. A warm glow of pride spread through me, fancy anyone dedicating a book to me—me, who was no one in particular, just a badly handicapped little Cockney girl. 'You've written about the treatment of cerebral palsy and one day I'll write about life in the unit,' I boasted, knowing that, although I wanted to write a book, at that stage it was little more than another of my wonderful pipe-dreams.

Mrs. Collis smiled, 'I believe you will. It's a story that you and no one else can tell.'

The 27th of November was John's birthday and on that day every year we had a big party with all the good food and sweets provided by his mother. If she was unable to bring them herself she used to send them by post and this year was no exception. We had a bigger than ever party—there was jelly and fruit; sandwiches of paste and jam; delicious little cakes coated with pink and white icing; and then the big birthday cake.

Outside the sky was dark and grey, rain came down in torrents, but inside everyone was laughing and happy, although one or two who had eaten well but perhaps not wisely, were feeling just the tiniest bit sick.

Before tea we had seen six doctors accompany Mrs. Collis into one of the other rooms. This was a normal occurrence so we did not take much notice, but apparently this time something more than the usual inspection was taking place. Hardly had the tables been cleared from our feast when John was summoned into the presence of these knowledgeable men and I was asked to start walking in the same direction. John walked much more quickly than I could with the aid of the crab, so by the time I reached the door he had been interviewed and was coming out. He passed by without a word.

'Please come in, Vera,' came a voice from within.

I clung to the door handle for support and lowered myself carefully into the chair just inside the door. Sitting next to me was a doctor I knew very well. He was a large man—in fact, it seemed they were all large men, and I felt very small.

The doctors kept asking questions of Mrs. Collis, friendly but rather as if she were on trial. Her answers came back quick as a flash and she seemed unperturbed, or perhaps a little irritated by the apparent foolishness of some of them.

Occasionally a question was flung at me and the big man sitting beside me would say, 'Now, Vera, don't be nervous, don't be shy, answer the doctors' questions nicely. Relax, don't wobble.'

All this helped to make me more nervous; the more he said 'relax,' the more I wobbled. I thought of the jelly I had just eaten for tea and I wanted to laugh. Here was I sitting wobbling like a jelly—a strawberry-flavoured one, my face was so red! Little giggles welled up inside, but I dared not let them out for fear all these grand men would think I was mentally deficient. At last I was allowed to go and join John in the schoolroom, where we both collapsed in hysterical laughter.

One outcome of this conference was an addition to the staff, a physiotherapist named Miss Greenfield-Brown. She was a lovely young lady, beautifully dressed and well spoken. Her hands were firm yet gentle and under Mrs. Collis's guidance she soon became invaluable in the unit.

About this time it became apparent to Mrs. Collis that unless I had an official job I would soon have to leave the unit. There was only one teacher allowed in each ward of the hospital and the work I did in the schoolroom was not recognized by the hospital authorities. There was only one way out; I was given a green overall and told I was an orderly. There was no pay attached to this job, but I did get free board and lodging and my treatment continued, so I was quite satisfied. The only house-work I did was to clean and tidy my own room, but there were numerous other tasks for which I was responsible and these included supervising the younger children while they took their rest-hour after dinner and helping in the schoolroom as before.

Another task was to keep an eye on the children in church and see that they did not misbehave. John sat with the few boys we had on the left-hand side of the church, while I sat with the girls on the right. The church was about half a mile from the unit and was reached by a very pretty walk through a long avenue of Canadian plane trees. We made a strange procession along this avenue—a row of orderlies pushing wheel-chairs, each containing two or three children.

In church each badly handicapped child was placed next to one who could hold a book. In this way everyone could take part in the service; but there was one pretty, golden-haired, blue-eyed little girl, who always sat next to me, not because she was badly handicapped but because she was such a little terror. If she sat next to another girl she would either tease or make her laugh. Another game she loved to play was to drop her collection money on the floor with a clatter, just when everyone else was very quiet. It was no use punishing her, she took no notice, so the only alternative was to ignore her. When she found she had no audience she soon learned to behave.

After church and until dinner-time John and I played our favourite game of make-believe. I would sit in the wheel-chair with John on the step at my feet while we pretended to be king

94

and queen of a desert island. This game consisted mainly of setting difficult tasks for our imaginary subjects to perform and allowed us plenty of scope for our vivid imagination, but we made sure we chose a secluded spot for our game in case we should be discovered by the younger children who might have thought it was childish to play such games at our age.

On Saturdays, when there was no school, John spent his time writing home. For him as for most of us this was a laborious task which took several hours. While he was busy I stayed in the schoolroom to watch and help the children at their play.

The schoolroom on Saturdays was a children's paradise. There were two or three small see-saws and one very large one; a Wendy house (a doll's house large enough for children to walk around inside); motor cars and tricycles of all shapes and sizes; big and small dolls' prams; dozens of dolls and small mechanical toys and books and puzzles of all kinds. There was also a very large mat-slide, but this was only used under supervision during eurhythmy.

Each child chose the toy most suited to his physical handicap, firm favourites being the tricycles and motor cars on which they could ride in and out of the french windows and around the whole block, instead of just staying in the schoolroom. At play the children were relaxed and happy and at first glance might almost have been mistaken for normal children. None of them wore splints or leg-irons. One Saturday morning the medical superintendent came in with a distinguished visitor who glanced around the schoolroom and with a puzzled frown was heard to remark, 'But, Doctor, you said these children were all badly handicapped. It is obvious that there is not much wrong with those here.'

'No?' queried the superintendent. 'Just call any one of them and ask them to do some trivial act that a normal child would do without even having to stop to think and then you will see the difference. Very few of these children riding tricycles at such speed can walk, and almost everyone here has a speech difficulty.'

95

I Become a Person

The visitor, subdued, left without realizing that he had been paying us all a compliment. To feel that we looked normal was the thing we all wanted more than anything in the world.

In spite of the fact that there were so many toys to play with sometimes the children preferred games of make-believe and I always took these opportunities to teach them something about the outside world. If they suggested 'a day at the seaside' we would sit in rows, as if in a railway carriage, and I would make train noises and give a description of the scenery we were passing. Another of their favourites was 'hospitals', but now it was different from the days when I first went to the unit. There were no longer any nurses around for them to copy so they played the game as any normal child would do, just for fun and without all the grim detail that used to make their game.

I had known most of these children a very long time and had grown very proud and fond of them. Their personal needs were well catered for at the unit, they received good schooling and treatment, but they also needed love. Some of them rarely saw their parents, as they came from homes all over the country, and so I did my best to give them the affection they needed and to show them that someone was really interested in what they did. This role earned me the title 'Old Aunt Vera'!

As in all families there were occasional fights between the children. If the opponents were of the same age and similarly handicapped I did not interfere, but if the trouble was between a big and a small child, or a boy and a girl, or two children with very different handicaps, then I would separate them and take one on each knee and ask them what the trouble was. Very often it was due to an accident—a wayward arm or foot had shot out and hurt someone or had broken a well-loved toy, but usually these quarrels were soon ended with a kiss and 'I'm sorry'. On those rare occasions when a child was really naughty and would not apologize then he was suitably punished, but first I made quite certain who was the real offender as I well remembered the day so long ago when I was put to bed for a week for fighting with another girl.

9

The First Step

Life was now running smoothly in the unit. Attention was paid to every detail of our lives and the days were full and happy. Miss Wood used my little room by day for helping us with speech, but I did not mind this as she was only there till 5 o'clock and her pictures brightened the walls. She also used a large mirror for her work and this was very useful to me when dressing in the mornings. It was impossible not to see myself when I got out of bed and so I began to take pride in my personal appearance. After many painful attempts I at last learned to comb my hair and get a resemblance to a parting. Very often my head received a terrific bump with the back of the hairbrush instead of the bristles, for the simple reason that the handle of the brush was polished and it therefore slipped around in my hand. Also, the comb often missed its mark and left a deep scratch in my face or neck, but gradually, with Miss Kember's aid, I learned how to attend to this part of my toilet and found I had mastered one more step to independence.

Miss Wood was very interested in spiritualism and we often spent hours discussing this subject. From her I learned a great deal and although there is still a lot I do not understand I did discover that a belief in spiritualism can be very helpful in contacting other people.

About a week before Christmas I slipped and fell in the treatment-room and in an effort to regain my balance I fell clumsily on my left foot, crushing it beneath me. Pain shot up my leg and involuntarily I screamed. Mrs. Collis came rushing in with the doctor who happened to be in the unit at the time.

'What have you done?' she gasped.

'I don't know, but it hurts,' I sobbed.

Calmly the doctor lifted me from the floor. 'Mrs. Collis, please hold Vera's foot, I think she has sprained her ankle.'

He was right. It was a bad sprain and for weeks it had to be kept strapped up with an elastic bandage. This meant that I could not practise walking and naturally no further progress was made for a time.

Mum had planned to go away for Christmas that year so I was not looking forward to visiting day because I thought that if she knew about my ankle she might cancel her holiday or at least worry about me and so not enjoy herself. About half an hour before she and Gladys were due to arrive I somehow managed to put my boot on and lace it up tightly. I thought that if I stayed in the wheel-chair and did not try to walk, the ankle would be all right and no one need know anything about it. All went well until just before they were leaving when Gladys said, 'I had better put your things away for you. Come with me to see that I put them in the right place.'

There was nothing for it but to hobble along beside her.

'What's wrong with your ankle, Vera?' she inquired. 'You are walking very badly today.'

'There is nothing wrong; Mrs. Collis is just trying some new treatment on me,' I lied, and this seemed to satisfy her, until the next visiting day when she discovered the truth.

After this incident Mrs. Collis decided it was time I learned to fall correctly so that I would not hurt myself in future. She explained that professional acrobats and parachutists fall regularly without ever hurting themselves, simply by relaxing their bodies and not tensing themselves against a fall. Soon I was falling down every day as part of my treatment, and when I had learned to do this correctly the fear of falling disappeared, and this gave me greater confidence for walking.

The First Step

Mrs. Collis was getting rather worried because I just could not manage to walk alone, although I had learned very quickly to walk on skis and to walk with the crab. The crab had never been my favourite way of walking because it took so long and it was boring; I much preferred to walk pushing a wheel-chair.

However, Mrs. Collis persevered and tried many different methods of teaching, one of which proved to be far more effective than any of the others. This was called the 'ski-slide' and was a board, made by our carpenter, into which the skis could be fitted. The idea was to walk up and down the board by sliding my feet forward and backward. When I had mastered this Mrs. Collis tied a length of webbing around my waist and then walked to the end of the room holding the other end of the webbing. She wound up the webbing as I walked towards her, rather as though I was a dog on a lead! This went on for some time, but still I was unable to walk alone.

It was thought a pair of crutches might help, but with them I was afraid of falling and hurting myself, so for this reason I walked very badly, very badly indeed. Mrs. Collis kept repeating, 'Tighten your bottom, Vera, stand up. You look like a bandy-legged cow!'

The tearful Vera would stand upright while Mrs. Collis was in the room but would soon go back to the old position when left alone. I was tearful because I wanted to do my best for the woman who had been so good to me, but everything seemed to be going wrong. There were times when I didn't want to walk at all, I was so tired of people saying, 'When you can walk we will do "so and so".'

After a week with the crutches they were taken away and I was given a pair of walking-sticks. With these I felt much happier because when I fell over the sticks could be quickly thrown aside and I did not fall on them.

I had been given a desk diary for Christmas and conscientiously kept it up to date with little everyday happenings. Now, one Monday in June, I proudly entered 'Walked on crutches'.

The First Step

The following Monday, 'Walked with sticks'. At the end of that week Mrs. Collis gave me a little pep talk.

'I am going away for a month's holiday and I want to see you walking on your own when I return,' she said.

Not very hopefully, I replied, 'I'll try.'

On the Monday after Mrs. Collis had gone away I went to my room after tea and sat on the floor to fill in the diary for the past week. The first six days were filled with trivial incidents, but there seemed to be nothing to write for the seventh day. Seeking inspiration I flicked the pages back for the past fortnight, and read 'Walked on crutches'. 'Not very well,' I thought. I turned the page and read, 'Walked with sticks.' 'How I wish I could put "walked on my own",' I mused, and on an impulse, added to myself, 'Why not try?' Without more ado, I put the book on the floor and pushed the wheel-chair outside into the courtyard.

I could not take the crab as I wanted to go on the grass, far from everybody. Pushing the wheel-chair I walked over the bumpy grass and then crawled about ten yards away from the chair, so that when I fell I could not hurt myself. Slowly I stood up, waited a moment to steady myself, and then moved the left foot forward—now the right one—down I went! I got up and next time went three steps before sitting down. For the first time in my nineteen years I had walked a few steps unaided. Overwhelmed with joy I cried like a baby. At that moment I wished more than anything else that Dad had still been alive to see me walk. He would have been so proud. Perhaps he did see me from the place where he had gone, and putting my hands together I thanked God for the miracle he had wrought in me that day.

Pushing the wheel-chair I walked back indoors and decided not to tell anyone what had happened in case they did not believe me, as I could not show them yet.

'Until I can walk ten steps I will not tell anyone, not even John,' I said to myself.

Luckily the weather kept fine for a few days and each night,

The First Step

after supper, I practised on the grass. John kept asking why I looked so happy, but I would not tell him as I wanted to keep the secret a little longer. By the week-end I could walk ten steps without falling, so after supper on Saturday I confided in John. I told him, 'I can walk ten steps by myself now. Don't tell anyone yet, will you?'

His eyes widened and his mouth dropped open. 'I don't believe you,' he spluttered. 'I just won't believe you until I see you do it. If you can walk then show me after this meal.'

'I can only walk on grass,' I hedged, 'I have not tried walking indoors yet.'

'Well, if you can walk on unlevel ground you should certainly be able to walk on a good floor. Go on, Vera, get going,' he ordered.

I crawled from the table to the middle of the room and slowly stood up. Laboriously I took five steps forward and then fell over backwards. John seemed transfixed. 'Get up and do it again, I don't believe what I saw.'

Again I stood up, took a few steps, and collapsed. This happened about ten times and then, exhausted, I pleaded with John, 'Please, don't tell anyone, will you? I am not sure of myself yet, and I don't want anyone to know until I can walk the length of the schoolroom without falling over once.'

So every day, after tea, while the orderlies were putting the children to bed, I walked up and down the schoolroom. John and I kept our secret until the day Mrs. Collis returned from holiday.

The morning seemed to drag; I was so excited at the thought of showing Mrs. Collis how I had progressed while she had been away. At last it was time to go into the treatment-room, and with the aid of the walking-sticks I went in.

'Keep those sticks nearer to you,' called Mrs. Collis.

This was the moment I had waited for. Feeling very nervous and shaky I put the two wooden sticks on the table and with my arms outstretched I walked forward. My body was bent almost double and I had a very wide gait, my legs being about

eighteen inches apart. Each step took approximately two
minutes to make and carried me forward about two inches, but
I was walking and was delighted with myself.

Mrs. Collis was silent. I had expected praise, and looked at
her expectantly. Quietly she asked, 'How long have you been
walking on your own?'

'About a month. I started just after you went away.'

'It's not very good, is it? Never mind, now we will learn to
do it properly,' she said bluntly, and there and then the difficult
job began.

About three months later it was decided to make a film of
the unit, a film that could be shown to medical students to help
them in their study of cerebral palsy. For several days techni-
cians walked in and out of the various rooms, taking shots of
the children at eurhythmy, John eating his meals, and many
other day-to-day incidents. Then Mrs. Collis asked me to walk
in front of the camera, not very far, just across the room. By
this time I could walk fairly well alone when no one was around
but to walk in front of a camera with lots of people watching
was quite another thing. I tried and tried but just could not do
it. The harder I tried the more I wobbled and bent forward;
it was just not good enough. After falling over about five times
I gave up trying, and at last managed to get across the width of
the room. My posture was not very good, but I had done it,
and I got out of the room as quickly as possible. As soon as I
was alone I burst into a flood of tears, I was so ashamed. Why,
oh why was I so nervous of walking in front of other people?
It was a feeling I could not conquer and never have. It seemed
to stem from the days when I was small and everyone used to
say, 'When you can walk . . .' or 'You have got to walk'. How
I wished that they had forgotten about walking until I could
sit or stand properly and do all the other things that come
naturally before walking. Even little children had always said
when meeting me for the first time, not 'Why do her hands
shake?' or 'Why can't she talk properly?' but always 'Why is
that big girl riding in a pushchair, why can't she walk?' It was

as if everyone believed that if I could walk I would automatically be cured of all my other handicaps and become a normal person. Of course this was not so, but the psychological effect of all this childhood propaganda has never really worn off; and even today I have this same nervousness of walking in front of other people.

As a special treat for working so hard, Mrs. Collis arranged for me to go with her, Miss Greenfield-Brown and a little girl named Evelyn, to see the *Swan Lake* Ballet at Covent Garden. We sat in a box, and as the lovely strains of the familiar music drifted up to us my mind seemed to disentangle itself from its awkward body and float upwards into a world of grace and beauty. Oblivious of everything and everyone except the fairy-like figures on the stage below I watched enchanted as their graceful movements told the story of the lovely Russian princess who is changed into a swan.

Glancing at her programme, Mrs. Collis recognized the name of one of the ballerinas as that of a friend of hers, and during the interval she invited her to our box. As the beautiful young lady came in I felt that I must surely be dreaming. But no, she shook hands and talked animatedly for a few minutes and from that day my love of ballet became more firmly rooted than ever.

By now Mrs. Collis was in great demand to give lectures all over the country, and a few days after our trip to the ballet she asked whether I would like to accompany her on a visit to Great Ormond Street Hospital in London. I was delighted to be able to be of some service to her, and did not mind in the least sitting on the lecture-room platform to show the doctors and students how to go floppy, and then going through my routine movements. It was a wonderful experience being able to help in this way and to realize that such an interest was at last being taken in the treatment of cerebral palsy.

After a very interesting discussion we were given tea and taken on a tour of the hospital. The wards were lovely and many of the children were lying in their beds on the balconies, enjoying the autumn sunshine, but how I wished I could take all these little children back to Queen Mary's where they could look at the fields and trees instead of just gazing at chimney-stacks and roofs. On the tour we were accompanied by one of the head doctors of the hospital. He was a very kind man and later I discovered that he was one of the doctors who had taken such an interest in me as a child.

Our tour ended and we returned to Queen Mary's, which to me was 'home'. I had never been happier in my life than I was at this time. At last there seemed to be some meaning to my life —I had a job to do, a job that I enjoyed; I had my own little room, good food, firm friends and hope for the future.

Between breakfast and school every morning there was half an hour to spare, and during this time some of the children used to go into the treatment-room and lie on the floor while I helped them to 'give up stiffening'. One of the little ones would start the metronome and then they would all lie quietly, but not making an effort to be still because this would have made them stiffen. Some of them looked rather like little wriggly worms. Even while they did their best, their bodies seemed to twitch uncontrollably.

There were other children who all their lives had unconsciously tensed up in an effort to do things, and now they had great difficulty in 'letting go'. Before they could learn to use their bodies correctly they had to overcome their self-imposed stiffness. This meant that they had to go through the 'wobbly' stage before they could be taught to use their muscles in a relaxed manner. Of course, this treatment sometimes met with the disapproval of the mothers, who did not understand what was happening. All they saw was that the physical condition of their children appeared to be worse as their arms and legs, which had previously been stiff and unmovable, shot out in all directions. The wiser mothers soon discovered that this was a stage through which their children had to pass before they could make any real headway, and that it was only a matter of time—sometimes years—before the shakiness was overcome by the correct method and not by tightening the muscles against it.

After dinner each day the smaller children were taken to the dormitory for a rest while I sat with them to make sure they stayed on their beds. While they were resting there was nothing I could do except read, and often the room became so quiet that I fell asleep, too. This job became quite boring until the day when Evelyn developed whooping-cough. At first no one was sure whether it was whooping-cough or a bad cold, as she did not whoop or vomit, but it soon became clear what was wrong with her as one by one the other children caught the germ. Before long the whole unit (except myself) was ill, but the children were not kept in bed as most of them had the cough in a mild form.

One day, during the after-dinner rest hour, I sat quietly reading a sordid murder story when little helpless Teresa started coughing. Teresa was three years old but was as helpless as a new-born baby. She could do nothing for herself and could not even talk. I was always rather scared of touching her, as she seemed so fragile I was afraid my clumsy hands would crush her body as if it were made of finest porcelain. As Teresa continued to cough her face began to turn blue and I rang the bell for help. Seconds passed and no one came, and Teresa seemed to be in danger of choking herself. Something had to be done quickly so, offering a silent prayer to God for guidance, I crawled quickly to her cot and grabbed her jumper. As gently as possible I pulled her upwards and put my left hand behind her shoulders to support her. Her head rested on my left arm, and soon she got her breath back and regained her normal colour. The whole incident lasted only three or four minutes but was one of the most frightening experiences of my life.

For a few weeks the after-dinner rest hour became a nightmare for as soon as one child awoke from his sleep and started to cough all the others would join in. When this happened there was no need to ring the bell for help! The noise of their coughing must have been heard several wards away and was the signal for all the orderlies, Mrs. Collis, Miss Kember and anyone else who happened to be around, to come running in to sit the children up. I became quite used to pulling the babies up by their clothing and being the target when they started to vomit! It was a great relief when the crisis was over and once more I had control of a sleepy dormitory.

On Friday mornings Mrs. Collis gave lectures to the orderlies and as I was now an orderly I attended the lectures with the others. It took me about a quarter of an hour to walk to the office, so I always started in plenty of time and was usually in my place when the others arrived.

These lectures were given because it was important for those working in the unit to understand what they were doing. It was no good the children learning how to do things in individual work if they did not carry out the movements they had learned in everyday life. For this reason the orderlies were taught how to carry and wash and dress the children and take them to the toilet. To understand the difficulties confronting a cerebral-palsied child we were shown how a normal child develops, and then told how and why the cerebral-palsied child does not grow up like his normal brother or sister. We were also told about the emotions of cerebral-palsied children. Every child loves and hates, cries and laughs, but the cerebral-palsied child may show these things too much. He may laugh loudly and hysterically, he may love very deeply, and he may hate when he feels he has been slighted in some small way.

Many people believe that cerebral palsy just means a certain kind of handicap which they can see, but it really means a disturbance of the nervous system which you cannot see.

The orderlies asked many questions, one of which was to query why Mrs. Collis did not help all mentally deficient children. She explained that if a child was to live a normal life he must be of sufficient intelligence to think of the detail of his movement and use this knowledge in everyday life.

When the responsibilities of the day were over and the children were in bed, John and I used to sit in the deserted

The First Step

schoolroom to listen to the radio. One night John switched off the set and started talking about the hospital ghost. The part of the hospital which was then used by the unit had at one time been the Nurses' Training Centre, and the story goes that one of the sister tutors dropped dead while on duty, and her ghost —'the lady in grey'—had often been seen in what was then our schoolroom. After a while John said, 'We had better go in for supper.'

'All right, John, you go in, I'll follow in my own time. Please turn the lights off after me, as I do not like walking in the dark.'

A mischievous twinkle shone in John's eyes and he raced out of the schoolroom before me, switching off the lights as he went.

I was still sitting by the fireplace and my mind was full of the 'lady in grey'. I fell to the floor and crawled out of the dark room as quickly as possible—or quicker! John had also switched off all the lights along the corridor and I crawled through it like a wild thing. The thud, thud, thud of my boots along the stone floor sounded like footsteps coming behind me and made me crawl faster and faster. To say I was frightened is putting it mildly; I was terrified. At last I reached the dining-room and stopped to get my breath, and there was John sitting on the floor laughing and laughing as though he would burst his sides.

'Oh, Vera,' he gasped between chuckles, 'I never thought anyone's hair would stand on end when they were frightened, but yours did. I'm sorry if you don't like the dark!'

I saw the joke and laughed with him and we were both giggling uncontrollably when the orderly brought our supper.

John loved teasing me, but he always made up for it afterwards. Once when he said he had a sweet for me he put some salt in my mouth, and then gave me a bar of chocolate later. Of course, I teased him too, but the years we spent together were happy years. We had grown so close to each other, we were more like brother and sister than two patients in a research unit. John was so sincere and somehow he always seemed to know what I wanted—sometimes before I did myself. Then one lovely summer day as I was walking across the courtyard after rest-hour, half asleep as usual, I saw John coming towards me with his mother.

'Good-bye, Vera,' he said simply, 'I will write soon.'

I thought he was only going home for a holiday. It was not until the next day that Mrs. Collis told me that John had gone home for good. For a week I cried myself to sleep each night and then I decided to write to him. I could not get used to being without him. I missed John most after tea for this was the time we had always spent together either listening to the radio or talking. Instead of the evenings being something to look forward to they were now long and desolate. I no longer enjoyed going into the schoolroom so Mrs. Collis had the radio moved into my own little room and I tried hard to fill up my spare time by either painting or making fancy belts from coloured twine.

John and I still correspond, but we have never met since that day.

My Tricycle

For three and a half years I had been helping in the school-room, but I wanted to know the work from every side so it was arranged that I should give up schooling and help in the Occupational Therapy room instead.

The term 'occupational therapy' is normally used to describe lessons in weaving, sewing, knitting, making toys, and so on, but this is not the kind of occupational therapy that Miss Kember gave in those days. She spent her time in helping us to lead normal lives. She taught us how to wash, dress and feed ourselves, to comb our hair and attend to our personal needs, to do up buttons and bootlaces, and the thousand and one every day tasks that come naturally to normal people.

I had been trained by Miss Kember for years, but had never studied her way of training other people and there is a world of difference between doing a job oneself and teaching other people. Judy was not very pleased that I no longer helped in the schoolroom, but Miss Kember was delighted with my humble assistance and made the work most interesting.

The occupational therapy class was split into two groups—the children of school-age and the babies. There were six babies including two-year-old twins, Molly and Ann. Ann was much less physically handicapped than her sister, but was more mentally backward and it was difficult to teach her anything. Neither of the children was very bright and Molly was completely helpless in every way. She could do nothing for herself, whereas

Ann's physical handicap was so slight that at first sight she appeared to be normal.

I spent many hours trying to discover how intelligent Molly was but it was very difficult owing to the severity of her handicap. Ann had no sisterly affection for Molly and would not play with her or do anything for her. I felt very sorry for their mother who was a most attractive young lady, for these were her only children. Mrs. Collis explained to the mother that owing to the limited mental capacity of the twins there was very little point in keeping them in the unit, and it was not fair that they should occupy places which could be used to greater advantage by more intelligent children. It was a hard decision to make but the unit was at that time the only place offering comprehensive treatment to cerebral-palsied children, and there were hundreds on the waiting list.

We heard later that Molly and Ann had gone with their parents to South Africa where labour is cheap and it would not be difficult to find nursemaids to look after them.

Apart from the twins most of the children made good progress and it was gratifying to see them improving so much. Three happy months passed until one morning as I slipped out of bed I felt a sharp pain in my left wrist. It felt like a bruised muscle and I reported it to Miss Kember. The regular doctor was on leave, and the trouble did not seem serious, so Miss Kember said, 'Don't worry about it, Vera, it will probably get better by itself in a few days. Just go easy on it for a while.'

However, it did not get better and by the week-end I could not use the left hand at all. I could feed myself with the right hand, but could not pick up a cup, as to do this without spilling the contents needed two hands. The orderlies had to help when I wanted to drink and they also had to do up my buttons and bootlaces. I hated to be a nuisance in this way, but there was no alternative.

On Saturday morning Lily and Brian begged me to take them for a walk in the hospital grounds and although my wrist was still painful I thought that the exercise it would get from pushing the wheel-chair might help it to get better. Instead, it had the opposite effect and before we had gone far the pain became unbearable and we had to return to the unit.

By Monday tea-time the whole of my left arm was stiff and sore. Half-way through this meal our regular doctor walked in, came over to where I was sitting, and said, 'What is this I hear about your wrist? Show it to me, please.'

I showed her the painful swollen thing at the end of my arm. One look was enough for her. She said, 'Don't use it until I get back. Wash it as clean as you can and then go into your room and read.'

At five o'clock she was back again with a large roll of sticky plaster. 'I am going to bind up your arm, starting from the bottom of your fingers up to your elbow,' she explained, as she rolled up the sleeve of my jumper. 'How long has it been painful?'

'Almost a week,' I murmured.

'Oh, Vera, what a foolish girl you are to let it go on so long!' she scolded. 'Why on earth didn't you tell the relief doctor last week?'

'I didn't think it was serious,' I faltered, 'but please, Doctor, what's wrong with it? Have I bruised a bone or something like that?'

'No, you've got tenosynovitis in your thumb and I don't want you to move your wrist at all. I'm going to give you some aspirin now so that you'll have a good night's sleep, and then you must get used to moving only your right arm for a little while.'

I did not mind the sticky plaster and the pain was less now, but oh, how I hated having to be waited upon once again.

After a fortnight the sticky plaster was removed and the wrist appeared to be better, but a few days later it started to hurt again and the medical superintendent suggested it should be put in plaster of paris. I did not like this at all. The plaster was terribly heavy and when it had been put on it took all the week-end to dry. There was only one consolation; as I walked the arm did not unpredictably fly up into the air (as it still often did) because the weight of the plaster kept it hanging by my side.

I was not much use to Miss Kember in the occupational therapy room with one arm out of commission so I returned to the schoolroom for a while; and one morning, as I helped Brian with his sums, I glanced up to see the doctor crossing the court-yard carrying a sling.

'Good morning, Vera. I want you to wear this sling for a little while. It will help your wrist to get better.' My heart sank for with a sling I would be really handicapped.

'But, Doctor, if I wear that my balance will be wrong, and I won't be able to walk properly.'

'I can't help that, you must rest the arm,' she interrupted, and it was apparent that further argument was useless. The sling was put on and I wore it for the next three months.

Walking was very difficult at first because I had been taught to walk with my hands in my pockets (to overcome the ten-dency to stretch them out in front of me) and now I had to learn to walk carrying this heavy weight strapped around my neck.

To cheer me up Mum took me home for a few days. The hospital clothes that I wore were a bit babyish for a girl of twenty, so while at home I borrowed some of Gladys's things. On the Monday I dressed up in a pair of navy blue slacks and a wine-coloured short coat, and in place of the white sling Mum pinned a wine-coloured scarf around my elbow. It was the occasion of the silver wedding celebrations of King George VI and Queen Elizabeth, so Mum pushed me in the wheel-chair the four or five miles to St. Paul's Cathedral and then tried to find a good spot for us to see the procession from. Unfortunately, by the time we arrived the streets were packed and we found ourselves jammed against the wall at the back of the crowd. Soon a woman with a child spoke to Mum. 'Your girl will see nothing from where she is. Please let me take her to the front. I'll look after her.'

'I don't want her to get in a crowd, they might knock her over,' Mum replied, but the kind lady would not be put off and helped me out of the wheel-chair and on to the edge of the kerb where I sat down.

Before long the royal carriage came in sight and everyone cheered and waved. I was very excited as this was the first time I had seen any of the royal family, then suddenly I wondered what the King would think if he saw one of his subjects sitting down in his presence. I wanted to stand up but couldn't do so because of the crowds and the kind lady was holding her own little girl in her arms so she couldn't help me. The humour of the situation struck me—here was I with my arm in a sling, dressed in slacks and sitting on the pavement in the centre of London while the King and Queen, in all their grandeur, passed within a few feet. I burst out laughing and was still laughing when the crowd dispersed and Mum helped me back into the wheel-chair.

A few days later when I returned to the hospital Miss Kember came out to greet me. She seemed very excited as she took my arm and said, 'Come with me, there is something waiting for you in the schoolroom.' We walked in, each trying to be a little taller than the other, and neither of us speaking. We reached the schoolroom and stopped in front of something covered by several red blankets.

'Now pull the corner,' she chuckled.

I thought she was playing a joke on me, but I pulled and then could not believe my eyes. There stood a magnificent full-sized tricycle. Speechless, I wondered where it had come from, and then remembered an incident that had occurred nine months previously. I had been walking through the courtyard one day when, as usual, I fell over and had been surprised to feel a pair of strong arms picking me up and putting me back on my feet. The strong arms belonged to Mr. Paul Cadbury, one of the well-known family of chocolate manufacturers. Later in the day I had asked Mrs. Collis if it would be possible for me to have a tricycle as I did not want to be dependent upon other people when I went home, and she had replied, 'Would you be able to ride it if you had one?'

'Oh, yes, I rode one when I was small.'

'Then write a letter to Mr. Cadbury and ask him very nicely if he will give you one. He has offered to make us a gift.'

Shocked at her suggestion I had replied, 'But, Mrs. Collis, I couldn't write such a letter. In any case he doesn't know me, and I don't know him.'

'Oh, yes, he does know you,' she had smiled. 'He asked me who was the girl he picked up from the floor.'

I had written the letter, not very hopefully, and now, nine months later, here was this beautiful tricycle, my passport to freedom.

Joy gave way to sadness. Oh, yes, here was the tricycle, but how could I ride it with my arm in a sling? Impatiently I waited for the day when the plaster was to come off and at last the doctor gave her consent. Her instructions were, 'Go easy for a little while. Your arm has been resting for a long time and you mustn't give it too much work to do just yet.'

This was probably good advice but I could not stay away from the tricycle—or 'my bike' as it became known—and every evening I went into the little room where it was kept and practised getting on and off. At first it felt strange sitting in the saddle such a long way up from the ground and with no back-rest or support, but by the end of a week I felt more confident and wheeled the bike out into the courtyard to learn how to pedal and steer. Steering was easy, but pedalling was more difficult because my feet just wouldn't stay on the pedals. They would do one or two turns and then fly up into the air, and it took several minutes to get them back in position. Eventually it became easier and so long as I stayed on level ground I found I could control the bike, and my feet, quite well.

At the same time as I was learning to ride the bike Miss Kember was teaching me something about music and how to appreciate it. I couldn't play the piano myself and knew I never would, but Miss Kember was a good pianist and often played for about an hour, after which she would explain why she had played a particular piece of music and what it meant to her.

One day as we both sat by the piano the window opened and a man's head appeared. He was a young man, about twenty-five I estimated, dark and quite good-looking. I recognized him as Mr. Bjerkhoel, one of the students who was then taking a six weeks' course at the unit.

'Hello,' he said, with his Norwegian accent. 'What are you playing? May I come in and play with you?'

He climbed in through the window. Miss Kember got up from her seat.

'Can you read music?' she asked him.

'Not a note,' he answered cheerfully, 'but I can play most well-known tunes from memory.' He sat down and played and sang and laughed, and we all laughed, he was such a gay and happy person to be with. He reminded me of the ray of sunshine that had shone behind his head as he looked through the window.

Mrs. Collis worked late that night and before she went home she played the piano for a while. I sat listening to her when suddenly, in the middle of a tune, she stopped.

'Do you like that male student, Vera? I hope that one day he'll come and work with us.'

'I like him very much,' I answered truthfully.

'Well, if he will come and work with us he can help you, and in return you can teach him quite a lot about cerebral palsy.'

Soon Mr Bjerkhoel became a member of the staff and to my joy he worked with me. He told me something about himself. He had started on his working life as a newspaper reporter but had not been very happy in this type of work and had become a professional ice-skater. To help with his skating he had studied ballet-dancing and so now he was able to teach and show me the correct movements in ballet. Often he would leap into the schoolroom and pick me up in the air as though I were a ballerina—it was wonderful.

Learning to ride the tricycle properly was part of my work, and for this we went all round the hospital grounds and sometimes on the roads outside as well. I would pedal as fast as I could so that Mr. Bjerkhoel had to run to keep up; sometimes I thought of him as a pet dog running alongside me and sometimes as a sportsman in training.

The tricycle had been built especially for me with a slight sideways tilt to allow for the camber of the road, and this made it very difficult for anyone else to ride. A number of people had tried to do so without success and one day, as we came in through the hospital gates, one of the teachers called across from the other side of the road, 'Lend me your bike, Vera, to go home on.'

'Oh no,' I said, laughing, 'you couldn't ride it.'

'Why didn't you let her try,' whispered Mr. Bjerkhoel. 'I would love to see her fall off and roll all down the hill, she's so fat.'

I laughed to think how funny she would look and the next day I was laughing at myself in a similar situation. It was a Saturday morning and one of the orderlies came to my room and called out, 'The medical superintendent wants to see you in the schoolroom.'

'Please help me to the door of the schoolroom and then I won't keep him waiting.'

The orderly left me in the doorway and I saw that the medical superintendent had a number of men with him. I walked as well as I could while he told the visitors about all the good work that was being done in the unit. They were all looking at me and I was nearly up to them when down I went, on to my back with my feet in the air. I blushed to the roots of my hair. 'Thank goodness I'm wearing dark knickers,' I thought. The visitors stared, but the medical superintendent seemed unperturbed.

'You see, all the children know how to fall so that they don't hurt themselves,' he continued, just as if the tumble was put on specially for their benefit. 'May I help you, Vera, I know you haven't hurt yourself. Come and meet my friends.'

My leg was pulled unmercifully when the visitors had gone, but an even funnier thing happened one day soon after. As I walked towards the treatment-room I saw the hospital chaplain and put out my hand to shake his. Somehow I missed his hand and fell straight into his arms and he gave me a friendly kiss. Recovering quickly, I said, 'I'm sorry I can't stop to speak to you now, I'm late for my work.'

As I continued on my way one of the orderlies joked, 'Fancy throwing yourself at a man. I didn't know you were so fast!'

Our little unit was becoming quite famous and was gradually growing in size. Besides Mrs. Collis, Miss Kember and Judy, we now had Mr. Bjerkhoel and another Norwegian therapist, Miss Ellingsen. Miss Greenfield-Brown had married and had left the unit to live in the north of England and she planned to start a cerebral-palsy clinic of her own. Before she left she arranged that when she had started the clinic she would send for me to go and work with her, but for some unknown reason things did not work out as planned. More than anything else in the world I wanted to work with handicapped people so that I could help them in the same way as I had been helped, and for about three months I had been looking forward to the day when I could go north. Then, one day, Mrs. Collis told me that everything had fallen through, and once more I had a broken heart. Didn't anyone want a girl with a handicap? Surely I was of some use in this world, otherwise why had I been allowed to live so long? I could not go to college because of my handicap and now I could not have the job I wanted—in fact I could not have any job outside of the unit, and how much longer would I be allowed to stay there? Night after night I lay awake wondering what the future held. Would I ever work? Surely I could if only I were given the chance, and a small voice in my heart kept repeating, 'Help cerebral-palsied people, you know something about that. Help cerebral-palsied people.'

My Tricycle

Once again Mrs. Collis started combing the country-side not for a college for handicapped people this time but to find some-one who would give me a job. She believed as I did that I could work if only I were given the chance. She left no avenue unexplored but the result was always the same, she came up against a blank wall every time.

At Christmas 1948 I went home for a few days' holiday and while there Mum received notice from the medical superin-tendent to the effect that as I was almost twenty-one I would have to leave Queen Mary's and go to a women's hospital for incurables in South London. I was to go there on the following Monday morning. It had come at last, the bombshell I had dreaded so long. I knew a number of girls from Queen Mary's had gone to this hospital before me and I also knew that once they got there very few of them came out again. My fear of this place was so great that I had always said I would rather die than go there, I did not want to be classed as an 'incurable' for the rest of my life.

Mrs. Collis knew all about my fears and had kept me at the unit as long as she dared, but hospital rules cannot be broken indefinitely and, after all, Queen Mary's was a children's hospital.

Although I had known for so long that one day I would have to leave the unit, that letter came as a great shock. I had thought that I was just going home for a few days for Christmas and I little dreamt as I said, 'Happy Christmas' to the people who lived and worked on the unit that this was farewell. I had said, 'I'll be back in a fortnight,' but now I knew I would never go back.

As I lay in bed that night my being was filled with despair. I thought of the unit and the fun I had had there, of how Mrs. Collis had worked and how I had done my best to help her. Surely she had not worked so hard with me just for me to spend the rest of my days in a home. 'Oh, God,' I prayed, 'if I have no purpose in life, if I cannot help someone somehow, then what is the use of going on living? If I am no use to anyone please take me home with you. I don't want to be a burden to anyone. Please don't let me spend the rest of my days in that horrible place.' My pillow was soaked with many tears before I at last fell into an uneasy sleep.

II

The Dark Days

The following morning Gladys went to see the medical superintendent and tried in vain to persuade him to change his mind about the transfer. He made it quite clear that because of my age I would have to leave Queen Mary's and the particular hospital I was to go to was the only one prepared to take me.

Mrs. Collis was sympathetic but had to bow to higher authority. However, before giving her consent she insisted on seeing the place and that afternoon, with Gladys, she went on a tour of the women's hospital. They were met by the matron who conducted them through the wards. Most of the patients were old ladies known as the 'chronic sick'. For them there was no cure and their faces seemed to reflect the knowledge that life now was just a matter of time, maybe years or only days, before death released them from their waiting. Interspersed among these old women were a few younger ones, most of them not physically ill but incapacitated by some disease or misfortune to such an extent that they were practically helpless. They looked forward to a future of perhaps twenty, thirty, or even forty years of lying in bed and being waited upon hand and foot. They appeared to be resigned to their fate—for them there was no alternative. Some of them had been in hospital all their lives, while others had lived at home until they had become too great a burden for their families, and then this hospital had been the only place to which they could go. They were well cared for and the nurses were kind, but to a stranger entering the wards the shadow of death seemed to hang like a grey mist—not only death as the end of life, but a living death where bodies breathed and ate and occasionally talked, but had no future and no hope except of fulfilment in the life hereafter.

Gladys was depressed by the place and walked silently through the long wards in the wake of Mrs. Collis and the matron. As the tour ended Mrs. Collis turned to the matron and expressed the opinion that this was hardly a suitable place for young women who, although handicapped, were quite well physically. Matron naturally resented this remark and regarded it as a slight on her running of the hospital. She bristled; how dared anyone interfere in her domain!

'Who is this Vera Dean that so much fuss should be made of her?' she demanded. 'What's so special about her? These women are treated very well here, and Vera should think herself lucky that she has got such a place to come to.'

On the way home Mrs. Collis confided in Gladys, 'Although I don't think that hospital's a suitable place for Vera it's much better than some I've seen and quite honestly is better than I'd expected.'

'Good Heavens,' thought Gladys to herself, 'if that's better than some other places, what must they be like?'

The week-end passed under an aura of gloom until Monday morning when Mum and I were taken by ambulance to my new home. With a few parting words of cheer Mum left and I was taken into the large day-room to dinner. Here those women who were allowed up sat around in wheel-chairs and had their meals. The time was 11.30 a.m. and although few patients had much appetite at this time of day, dinner was always served at this early hour to allow the staff to take their midday meal at either 12 or 1 o'clock.

A number of young women were already seated around a long table and I was placed on a chair at the end. The women talked among themselves but no one spoke to me. I was too miserable to care much and picked at the unappetizing meal set before me. For two or three days I felt like an outcast. No one spoke to me, and when I tried to talk to them they didn't seem to understand what I was saying. Probably a great deal of this isolation was my own fault; I was frightened of them and rather afraid of my new surroundings. Everything was so different from the gay and happy atmosphere that had prevailed at the unit. Most of these women had already been here for years and had become used to the dull routine. They were happy enough in their own peculiar way and could not understand why I disliked the place so much.

'You've been spoilt all your life, that's the trouble with you,' one young woman sneered. 'Don't think you can come here and do just as you please. We've been here for years and don't get many privileges, so you needn't think that you can do just as you like!'

Most of the women slept in the wards, but there were a few small side rooms and I was given one of these to share with a girl named Betty. She was about thirty-five years of age and we took an instant dislike to each other. For years Betty had had this room to herself, and she resented having to make room for me—a mere child, as she thought. Her pet phrase was, 'It's no use trying to explain to you, you wouldn't understand.'

I was told to go to bed each night at 5.30 p.m. and stayed there with nothing to do but sleep until 7 a.m. next morning. I could not carry things and walk at the same time, and I did not like to keep on asking the women to fetch and carry for me. Betty used to go to bed at 6.30 p.m. and then put on her earphones and bring out her needlework. Not a word would pass between us until 8 p.m. when we were tucked down for the night.

Betty was always up early but one morning I woke as she was dressing and was surprised to see that she had no feet. She always moved around in a wheel-chair and until that morning I had had no idea why she could not walk. Fascinated, I watched as she put on her boots.

'Were your feet cut off very long ago?' I asked. 'I think you are clever to be able to keep your legs in boots.'

The Dark Days

Startled into the realization that she was being watched, Betty turned to me. 'How dare you look at me!' she cried. 'Turn over and go to sleep again, and don't be such a peeping Tom.'

Every day was exactly the same as the one before; the only break in the monotony was at visiting times and on Sunday mornings when the Girl Guides came and took us to church. This was an occasion to be looked forward to, not so much because I enjoyed going to church but because for an hour or so I was in company of girls of my own age who laughed and chatted and were glad to be alive.

Each day, after breakfast, we went into the recreation hall where we sat until dinner-time. We each had our own particular chair in our own particular place and the 'new girl' could not choose where she would sit. For dinner we went into the day-room and then back to the recreation hall until tea-time, after which we went to bed.

Most of the women did needlework or crochet during the hours we spent in the hall. They bought the materials from the occupational therapist who came every day, but like so many people she did not want to see her materials wasted and for this reason she refused to give me anything to do.

Whenever I approached her she would say, 'What can you do? You can't knit or sew, so what can you do?'

There was nothing to do but read, and life became very dull. The only relief from boredom during these days was to ride round and round the large hall on my bike. As a special concession I had been allowed to take my bike into the hospital and keep it in the recreation hall where I could ride it whenever I chose. The scenery on these trips round and round was not very inspiring, but it did afford an opportunity to stop and speak to some of the more friendly women.

After a fortnight of idleness the occupational therapist was persuaded to give me about ten yards of macramé twine to make a belt. This was nowhere near sufficient, as it takes about sixty yards of cord to make a belt, but I thought I would at least make a start with this and show her I could do something properly. However, I was so nervous I got the cord into an awful muddle, and she had to unravel it, much to her disgust.

'If I've got to stay in this place for years and do nothing but sit in this recreation hall every day, looking at a lot of miserable faces, I shall go mad!' I burst out at her. 'There's another woman here with cerebral palsy and she makes really lovely woollen rugs, so why won't you teach me to make one of those?'

'No, you'll never make anything like that,' she insisted, 'you'd only waste the materials.'

When Mum came to see me she had an argument with the occupational therapist because of her attitude, but it did not help; she just didn't have time to teach me anything, so Mum brought some canvas and wool from home and I taught myself to make rugs by copying the other girls.

One morning I received a letter from Mrs. Collis in which she suggested that I should try to help some of the other girls with cerebral palsy by giving them the benefit of the knowledge I had gained at the unit. Whenever I found myself alone with one of them I would try first to diagnose the type of handicap with which she was afflicted and then devise the form of treatment which would suit her best. I told them about Mrs. Collis and explained her work, but none of the girls would listen to me until Hazel, who was about twenty-eight, said, 'Show me this wonderful new treatment of yours.'

'Please sit in the armchair, Hazel—the floor's rather dusty—and pretend you're a cat relaxing in front of a fire.'

She did as she was bid while I took hold of her arm and started moving it gently up and down. Hazel could walk after a fashion, but her arms were practically useless to her because they curved in an arch above her head. With an effort she could put them down by her sides, but before long tension would draw them back into their unnatural position. For a few moments Hazel allowed me to move her arms, but suddenly she must have thought she looked ridiculous, for she sat bolt upright in the chair and cried, 'You don't know what you're talking about! I've had a lot of treatment which hasn't done me any good at all and I don't see how your silly idea can help me or anyone else.' She hobbled out of the room and went straight to the other women, saying, 'Don't take any notice of Vera. She's got some funny ideas.'

Hazel had quite an influence on the other women and so naturally they listened to her. I felt dreadfully hurt for, after all, I was only trying to help the girl and she certainly needed help; but after this episode none of the other women would even listen to me, so I gave up the idea of trying to help them. Their attitude to life was that there was no hope for them in this world and the only thing they looked forward to was to die and go to heaven.

On Mondays only those women who could dress themselves —about four or five of us—were allowed to get up. I often wondered why this was so until one day I discovered that Monday was bath-day for the more handicapped women, and they were kept in bed so that the staff would not have the work of dressing them twice in one day.

My bath-time was Thursday at 12.30 p.m. when I was taken to the bathroom by two nurses. I was undressed by them and washed and was not left alone for a second. At the unit I used to enjoy a bath and looked forward to the moment when I could lie back and let the water lap gently over my shoulders, but now this was taboo; whenever I tried to lie back in the water the nurses seemed to be under the impression I was trying to drown myself. I was watched the whole time and felt like a murderess awaiting execution. As soon as the bath was finished, at about 1 p.m., I was put to bed and stayed there until 7 next morning.

Although I had left the unit, Mrs. Collis was still interested in my progress and shortly before my twenty-first birthday I was taken by ambulance to her advice clinic.

'Hallo, Vera,' she greeted me, 'how do you like your new home?'

'Not much,' I grunted. 'My mother's trying to get a ground-floor flat so that I can go home to live, and I hope she gets it soon.'

'Yes, I know about the flat, and we'll do what we can to help.'

I felt at ease sitting there listening to her talking once again, and she continued: 'Now you're twenty-one I'll give you the key to your life. I have taught you all I know about cerebral palsy. I shall probably go on finding out more and more about the details but you know the principal facts. I can't help you any more at this time because I don't know anything that you don't know yourself. You'll find many people who think they know all about you and will tell you what to do, but be patient with them and try to teach them the truth, which only a few people know, and you are one. You'd better go back to the hospital now, but don't despair; it probably won't be for long.'

As the ambulance driver helped me out from the clinic, Mrs. Collis called, 'Use that key well and you can help other people and yourself, but if life gets a bit too hectic, I will help you.'

On Friday evenings the local Girl Guide Captain came into the hospital to hold a Land Ranger meeting in the recreation hall. For years I had secretly longed to be a Girl Guide, but had always thought this was impossible until I learned of the branch of the Guiding movement known as 'the extensions' or 'Post Rangers and Guides', which caters for those girls who are too badly handicapped to attend ordinary meetings. There is also a similar movement for the Boy Scouts. For those Post Rangers and Guides who live at home the 'meetings' usually take the form of a magazine which is sent through the post to their homes, each member of the company in turn adding some item of interest.

At these Friday evening meetings we had a great deal of fun, playing games and learning about the Guiding movement, and Captain often told us about camp and the wonderful time we would have there. As we sat listening to all her exciting stories I was enthralled but never dreamt what Guiding would mean to me in the years to come.

After I had been in the hospital for about a month I discovered by chance that if Mum applied for a pass she would be allowed to take me out on Saturday afternoons. I could not go home as the pass was only operative until 6 p.m., but it did give a chance to get outside the hospital and among normal people for a few hours. Mum and Gladys took advantage of this concession every Saturday and we used the time either to go to the local cinema or to go cycling on the Common. All the week long I looked forward to Saturday afternoons and would watch the hands of the clock crawl around until they reached two. From two till six was like being in another world, but all the time I was enjoying my outing a nagging voice kept saying, 'Don't let this afternoon end. Don't let it be six o'clock for a long time yet. I wish I didn't have to go back.' I was not ill-treated in the hospital, I was simply bored and lonely.

One Saturday morning at the end of February a nurse came to me and said, 'You will have a visitor this afternoon. A young lady has just called here to see you and has gone to do some shopping until visiting time.'

'Who was she?' I inquired.

'I couldn't understand her name, it was something foreign,' answered the nurse.

During dinner I racked my brain. A foreign young lady, who could it be? Well, I would know soon. I sat by the window and watched the people walking up the drive to see if I could recognize anyone and then—there she was—it was Judy, my Judy. I hadn't thought of Judy because she was English, but she was married to a Dutchman and presumably that was why the nurse could not understand her name. I was overjoyed to see her again and we talked for some time before Judy paused as if to make some important announcement.

'Vera,' she said slowly, 'I have come here specially to see you today because I am leaving the unit.' Her voice was happy and yet tinged with a note of regret as she continued, 'I'm going to have a baby. My husband has got a new job at Cambridge and we are moving there soon. I shall hate leaving the unit and all our children, but it will be lovely to have a baby of my own. You know I've always wanted a family.'

I was happy for Judy and wished her joy, but I could not help feeling a little sorry for the children at the unit who would soon be losing her. To most of them she was the only teacher they had ever known and more than that, she was a very dear friend. She had loved all the children almost as if they had been her own and had always been so proud when one of them had accomplished some new task. Dear Judy, I wondered who would take her place; whoever it was would have a tremendous job to capture the love and loyalty of the children as she had done.

'I'm sorry I can't stay long,' Judy's voice arrested my wandering thoughts, 'I have to catch a train, but I dare say your mother will soon be here.'

'Oh, yes, she'll be here at two o'clock,' I replied. 'Oh, it's almost two now. If you'll help me into the recreation hall I'll get my bike and cycle down with you to the hospital gates.'

As we went down the drive Mum and Gladys came towards us, screwing up their eyes to see who was the young lady with me. They smiled as they met and exchanged a cheery greeting. After a few minutes of happy gossiping Judy looked at her watch. 'Well, Mrs. Dean and Gladys, it has been lovely to see you again, but I really must go. Do tell me, though, how are you getting on with your flat-hunting?'

Mum smiled. 'I had a letter from the L.C.C. this morning to look over a flat next Tuesday.'

I sat quite still on my bike, unable to believe my ears. Could this be true? Was it possible that the sun was beginning to show through the dark clouds? Judy interrupted my dreaming.

'Well, good-bye, Vera. I do hope you'll be happy and get on well. I feel much happier now that I know you'll soon be going home.' She walked down the road and out of my life, taking

with her a little of my heart and much of my gratitude for all
the help she had given me in the past.

The afternoon sped past, but when Mum and Gladys had
gone home the time seemed to drag. For the next two days I
could think of nothing else but the new flat. Would it be suitable, would Mum take it? I would not know the answer until
visiting time on Wednesday and I tried to think of other things,
but it was no use. I tried to read but the words meant nothing;
would the time never pass until Wednesday? In bed I lay awake
for most of the night thinking and praying. My thoughts strayed
between happy visions of the future in a new home and dark
despair at the thought that maybe the flat would not be suitable
and I would not be able to go home after all.

Eventually it was Wednesday and the hands of the clock crept
once more towards two. I sat at the end of the recreation hall
and as Mum walked towards me, she smiled. My heart bounded.
'I can't stay long today, Vera,' she said, as she kissed me.
'We're moving next week and there's a lot to do.'

Eagerly I asked her for details of our new home. It was a
three-roomed ground-floor flat on a new estate in Highbury,
North London, and it had a little balcony where I could sit in
the sun, and there was a yard where a shed could be erected to
house my tricycle.

As we talked I felt as though a great weight had been lifted
from my shoulders. After three dark months a curtain had been
drawn back and I could see the sun. For the next fortnight the
hospital staff kept remarking on the difference in me. From the
sullen crying girl I had been, I had become once again a cheerful, happy person with hope in the future.

On Mum's next visit she asked the sister if I could go home
on the following Wednesday. 'Of course,' the sister answered,
'but I know Vera will be back within two years, they always
are.' She didn't seem to like losing her patients, because she
kept telling me about all the fun we would have when I came
back to the hospital. She just could not realize how relieved I
was to be leaving.

The Dark Days

On Tuesday I was given a bath and put to bed until Wednesday afternoon when a nurse came in to dress me. For years I had dressed myself and felt thoroughly awkward while being waited on. I was also tremendously excited and the poor nurse had her work cut out to get me into my clothes by the time Mum arrived. Soon afterwards Mum and I were in an ambulance together with a small suitcase, containing my clothes and personal possessions; my wheel-chair and tricycle went with us, too.

'What do you think this is, a removal van?' quipped the driver, as he closed the doors behind us. I laughed, and a lump came into my throat. God had heard my prayers and I was leaving this place that I hated so much and going into a big, strange world. What did the future hold now, I wondered happily.

A number of the patients looked from the windows of their wards and waved, 'Good-bye, Vera,' they called, 'you're lucky to be going home. We wish it was us!'

Most of them knew that a moment like this would never come to them. Some of them who had spent all their life in hospital had never known what it was like to live in an ordinary home. To them the world was bounded by the hospital walls. For years they would go on eating and breathing, but they would never really know what it was like to live.

I felt a great pity for these women who were condemned to spend probably the rest of their lives in idleness; more so because most of them were capable of doing some form of light work if only they had been given the opportunity to learn.

The hospital gates closed behind us and the most miserable three months of my life came to an end. The sun was shining as I looked at the road ahead and suddenly the winter had passed and it was spring!

12

Home

The ambulance pulled up outside a large block of flats in Highbury. Mum got out and opened the door of a flat on the ground floor and I was taken inside. So this was our new home. How small it seemed after the spaciousness of the hospital and the unit. Everything was bright and clean, with gleaming new paint and freshly distempered walls, but oh how those walls seemed to bear in on top of me. I longed to pushed them back and have more space.

The flat was not over-furnished and yet after the bareness of hospital wards it seemed that there was furniture everywhere and I was in danger of falling over it every time I moved. I began to get scared. If I tried to walk and fell it was more than likely that I would hit my head on a table or chair and, quite apart from hurting myself, I would probably damage the furniture.

I looked around for some place where there was no furniture to fall on and discovered that the french windows in the sitting-room led on to the small veranda. Mum helped me through the windows; quite probably I could have walked through unaided, but the sight of so much fragile glass petrified me and turned my legs to jelly. 'One slip', I thought, 'and I'll smash about twenty panes of glass.'

It was peaceful sitting on the veranda in the pale spring sunshine. The view was quite pretty, too. To left and right were more blocks of flats, but directly in front was a large green lawn with colourful flower-beds dotted about and a few trees showing their first fresh green leaves. The lawn was bounded by a very low wall beyond which was the road where buses and cars passed.

I sat there for some hours, drinking in the newness of my surroundings, quite content to watch the few passers-by, until a new noise reached my ears. It was 4 p.m. and the children were home from school. They chased each other along the road and across the green lawn; they skipped and jumped and played ball; and then several of them turned and saw me. They stared. My appearance when sitting still is not so very different from that of a normal person, but perhaps an uncontrolled twitch of the head or a spot of saliva creeping down my chin in an unguarded moment had shown them that I was different. They were not quite sure how I was different, probably they had never seen a person with cerebral palsy before, but they knew that there was something wrong with me and they stared and stared.

Annoyed I called out to them, 'What are you looking at?' My gruff voice puzzled them even more than my shaky body. Then they started to laugh.

'She's potty,' yelled one small boy. 'Ya, ya, ya, look at that soppy girl!'

Angry and hurt I called to Mum to take me indoors. These were only children, and they didn't understand what was wrong with me; all the same, their words were cruel and made me bitter. It was bad enough to be handicapped and frustrated in so many ways, but to be ridiculed for that handicap was even harder to bear.

It was days before I sat on the veranda again and then the same thing happened. As soon as the children came home from school they regarded me first as an object of wonder and then as a butt for their cheeky comments. Mum tried to reason with them but received only abuse for her pains and gave up in disgust. Not all the children in the flats were such hooligans, but it needed only one or two of them to poke fun at me and the

Home

others soon followed suit. It was a new game to them, and no doubt they would have outgrown it in time, but Mum decided it would save a lot of unpleasantness all round if in future she took me out in the wheel-chair in the afternoons.

On these afternoon outings we sometimes went for a walk through the park but more often than not we met Aunt Queen, who lived near by, and went with her around the shops. Aunt Queen usually pushed my wheel-chair and quite naturally a number of people thought she was my mother. Often, while Mum was in a shop making a purchase, we would wait outside and someone would come up to Aunt Queen and inquire, 'How is your daughter today?'

'Very well, thank you,' Aunt Queen would reply with pride.

'What does she do all day?'

'She works in an office,' Aunt Queen would answer, referring to her daughter Sylvia. The inquirer's face would pucker into a puzzled frown, and we would realize that she was talking about me.

'This is not my daughter,' Aunt Queen would explain, laughing, 'her mother is in the shop, but if you want to know how Vera is, why don't you ask her? She's twenty-one, you know.'

Very often this remark would be followed by the person whispering something in Aunt Queen's ear, whereupon she would dismiss the person with the words, 'I've just remembered something my sister can get for me,' and march into the shop.

When she came out I would ask her, smiling, 'What made you so cross?'

'I don't know why people think you're silly, just because you're not so active as they are and your speech is poor. That person asked me if you could understand what we were saying, and she was surprised when I told her that of course you could.'

'Just let me hear anyone say that,' Mum would chime in, 'and I'll give them the right answer!'

Home

From the time I came of age I received a National Assistance grant of about twenty-five shillings a week. While in the women's hospital a pound of this had been retained by the authorities to help pay for my upkeep and I had been given five shillings a week pocket money. This I had always handed to Mum to buy with it the things I needed, but now that I was at home Mum drew the weekly allowance and gave me the five shillings to spend for myself. While we were out I would choose the things I wanted and Mum would purchase them, and when we came home I would try to sort out the right money to give her. 'Which', I would wonder, 'are the right coins?' I had forgotten the difference between shilling, florin and half-crown, and also between a penny and a halfpenny. It was so many years since I had handled any money that I had to look closely at the words on each coin to discover its value.

In hospital I had always risen at 7 a.m., but at home the routine was quite different. Gladys left for her office at 9 o'clock and Mum then woke me with breakfast in bed. About ten I would get up and wash and dress at leisure so that it was generally 12 noon before I was ready to face the world. For about an hour before lunch I helped Mum with the housework by washing and polishing the floors and sweeping the carpets on the days when the vacuum cleaner was not being used. These things I could do on my knees, but I never attempted to do anything like dusting, as I was so afraid of breaking things.

In the evenings we would sit with our handiwork; Mum with her crochet, making dainty little mats and doilies; Gladys with her needlework (she made most of our clothes); and me with several large balls of plastic twine, making belts. Each belt was made in a different pattern and Gladys had no difficulty in selling them to the girls at her office for five shillings each, but as it took a whole week to make one belt there was not much profit left after deducting the cost of the plastic.

Once a week we went to the pictures. There was only one cinema near by where we were allowed to take the invalid chair. If we wanted to go to any of the other cinemas the only way to get there was by bus. Mum and Gladys used to stand on each side of me and link their arms through mine and in this way we could walk to the bus stop. Usually we were in a hurry so as not to miss any of the programme and I had no time to walk properly. Instead of placing my heels firmly down on the pavement I moved forward with very jerky movements, putting only the toes on the ground and resting heavily on Mum and Gladys. I knew that I should not be walking in this way, using all the wrong movements and making a wrong pattern on my brain, but to walk properly it would have taken about an hour to reach the bus stop and we would have been too late to see the film.

For this and other reasons I became very unsteady when walking indoors and Mum unwittingly made things worse. She remembered the children she had seen at Queen Mary's who had spent years lying on their backs recovering from falls they had received at home, and the memory of these children made her anxious. 'Be careful not to fall over, I don't want you to hurt yourself,' she would say when I got up to walk. She was only trying to help, but the more she worried about me the more nervous I became, and the more often I fell over. When I was picking myself up she would say, 'Have you hurt yourself. You did frighten me!'

I told her there was no need to worry because I knew how to fall, but her comment was, 'I expect you do, but you might do it once too often.'

Gradually confidence in my ability to walk left me and I took to pushing around a small wooden chair when indoors. By holding on to the back of this I could stand fairly upright and walk from room to room. The legs of the chair made dents in the linoleum, but Mum minded this much less than seeing me sprawling on the floor after a fall.

She was disappointed because I seemed to be getting so much worse. During visiting times in hospital I had always been on my best behaviour and had never attempted to do anything that was difficult, and consequently Mum didn't really know what I was capable of doing. Mrs. Collis had told her that I could look after myself, but she had forgotten to add 'in her own way and in her own time'. I found life at home very difficult. Mrs. Collis had said that I never made a mess with food, but then we never had things like soup at the unit, in fact most of our food was rather dry. When Mum gave me a nice plate of soup and told me not to make a mess, I subconsciously thought that I would be bound to make a mess if I fed myself in the ordinary way; so I began to tense all the muscles of my body and as soon as I picked up the spoon I started to wobble. The more I wobbled the more mess there was on the clean white tablecloth, which of course didn't please Mum, and she would repeat over and over again, 'Since you left Queen Mary's you haven't bothered to try. Goodness knows I help and worry about you enough. What is the matter?'

I would try to mumble something like, 'You help and watch me too much,' but before the words were out I would always burst into tears. Mum couldn't bear to see this, so for years she stopped making things like soup, custard and milk puddings that were difficult for me to manage. Nevertheless, it took me a very long time to get used to the idea of having Mum sit at the same table at mealtimes, watching me eat. I somehow expected that she should have her meals in another room as the staff did at the unit.

When alone in my room I practised a certain amount of movement control, going through the routine movements I had learned so thoroughly at the unit, but I did not do this so often as I should have done. I felt self-conscious of practising in front of Mum because I was afraid she would criticize or not understand what I was doing, and I did not feel capable of explaining to her.

I was at that time a little afraid of Mum. For years we had no actual life together. She had visited me regularly in hospital, but in a way we were strangers to each other. Mum was inclined to treat me as her baby while I thought of her as being something like a ward sister. I asked for the things I wanted, but I could not tell her my thoughts. I agreed with everything she said because I dared not express my own opinions. Gladys and I have always been very good friends and have told each other our secrets, but it was a long time before I shared my hopes and fears with Mum. However, with patience and love I began to understand Mum and to think of home as home and not as a paradise. In hospital I had often dreamed of home as a small girl dreams of fairyland and it was not until I came home for good, instead of for just a holiday, that I realized that life even for normal people is not all milk and honey, and there are a great many things to worry about in this world that I had never known existed. For instance there were no money worries in hospital. Everything was provided and it never entered my head to wonder what a thing cost or who paid for it. At home I found that for Mum shopping was a real headache. She had a small widow's pension and with my allowance and Gladys's earnings we managed quite well, but only because Mum knew where and when to shop. She would tour the local markets just before closing time and would often come home with her basket full of fruit that she had bought at a ridiculously low price because the stallholders were anxious to sell out and go home.

One Sunday afternoon Gladys and I were sitting on the veranda when there was an unexpected knock at the front door. Seconds later Mum came out to us bringing with her a lady and gentleman.

'Here are some visitors for you, Vera,' she called.

The lady introduced herself. 'I'm Mrs. Gentry and this is my husband. I'm Divisional Commissioner for Guides for this area, and the Girl Guide captain at the women's hospital where you were has written to tell me that you would like to become a Ranger.'

She was such a friendly person and seemed to take such an interest in me that it was not long before we were talking as if we had known each other for years. Mr. Gentry, a very jovial man, stood leaning back on the french windows and made little jokes whenever he could get a word in. Suddenly there was a crash—he had fallen through the window! He looked so funny that we burst out laughing. Luckily he did not hurt himself, but he was terribly worried about the broken window and offered to come back next day with some glass to repair the damage. Mum persuaded him that this was not necessary as our next-door neighbour would soon fix it for us, and eventually he and his wife left with a promise to call again in a few days.

'Well, that's a good way to start a friendship,' Mum laughed when they had gone. 'He certainly broke the ice!'

A couple of days later Mr. and Mrs. Gentry called to take me to a Ranger meeting. As we walked towards their car I saw, as I thought, a little girl sitting in the back seat. The 'little girl' was Gwen who also suffered from cerebral palsy. She was actually two years older than me but she was very tiny and looked about ten years of age.

Gwen and I were taken to a church hall near by where an active Ranger company were holding their weekly meeting. I do not remember very much about that meeting, but the journey home stands out very clearly. We were driving along in the car and Gwen was talking about her typewriter, when I said, 'I wish I had a typewriter, then I could type letters to my friends. Writing takes such a long time.'

There was a pause, and then Mr. Gentry asked, 'Do you really want one, Vera. I've an old typewriter in my office which isn't used much. Would you like it?'

'Oh, yes, please!' I answered delightedly.

Mr. Gentry delivered the typewriter a few days later and I had quite a shock. It had a twenty-four-inch carriage and was a German make, so it had a few additional keys to those found on an English machine. Gladys is a shorthand-typist but she didn't like using this typewriter very much as it seemed rather heavy to her. However, it suited me down to the ground. I could bang as hard as I liked and no damage would be done. I used two fingers to type with and at first the result was an awful mess, but soon it improved and I was able to write little letters to my friends. One of my greatest difficulties was spelling. Because of my defective speech I could not pronounce words properly, and consequently I spelt them as I thought they sounded. The results were sometimes quite weird and Gladys had many a good laugh when looking through my efforts. To improve my spelling, and to help my friends to know what I was talking about, Gladys used to read through all my letters and correct the spelling mistakes and then give them back to me for retyping. Sometimes she would give them back two or three times if the typing was very poor, and so it often happened that a letter I started writing on Monday didn't get posted until the week-end.

It was at this time that I started typing the first chapter of this book, but for some reason or other it didn't go well and I didn't touch it again for years.

Every week Gladys or one of the Rangers took me in the invalid chair to the meeting in the church hall and there Gwen and I would watch the girls in their various activities. Gwen and I became very good friends and soon she earned herself the nickname 'Wobbles', because, although she could walk, she wobbled quite a lot and often fell over. Gwen was also handicapped by deafness in one ear so I had to listen very carefully to what was going on and then tell her afterwards. The more I knew Gwen the more I liked her and I used to look forward to going to Rangers. It was the only time I could say what I liked. Normally, in company, Mum and Gladys did all the talking and I sat and listened—it used to annoy me sometimes when we were out and met one of my Ranger friends; they did all the talking, and I could not get a word in edgeways—but at Rangers there was nobody to speak for me so I had to speak for myself. Whenever I see a square hall, brightly lit, my mind goes back to those evenings and the fun we had—the girls marching, the big Girl Guide parades, the games we played and the songs we sang. Whenever you get a dozen Rangers together you are transported into another very happy world.

Home

When I had been home for about eighteen months the Ministry of Labour sent me notice to attend at a hospital about twenty miles away to see if I was fit for employment. No transport was provided so Mum asked Aunt Queen to come with us and we went there by bus.

I looked forward to the interview because I thought it would open the door of a training college to me. I had visions of becoming a typist or a dressmaker, not because I wanted to become a typist or a dressmaker but because I thought the knowledge would be useful when the time came to help cerebral-palsied people. However, now that I sat in front of the small bald-headed man who was chairman of the committee, I found these visions were just another pipe-dream. The bald-headed man addressed all his remarks to Mum—I believe he thought I was incapable of opening my mouth, or was half-witted.

'Now, Mrs. Dean, what can your daughter do?'

'She can make very fine knotted belts and she is beginning to use a typewriter. She is not very expert just yet but she is improving.'

'Can she knit or sew?'

'No, not yet. The specialist at the hospital told her she was not ready for those things.'

The doctors took one look at me and announced, 'We are very sorry, Mrs. Dean, your child will never be able to earn her own living and it is no use trying to train her to do something at home because she will never be capable of doing anything.'

All this time Aunt Queen, who was sitting beside me, was getting redder and redder in the face. Eventually she could stand it no longer and she spoke her mind. 'I've known Vera since she was a baby, and I know the progress she has made with very little schooling. She can read and type and while she was in hospital she was trained, so why can't she be trained now?'

The answer to this was, 'We've tried to train people like Miss Dean before, but it's a waste of time. Good afternoon.'

Home

A very cross aunt caught hold of my arm and said, 'Come on, Bert (Mum's nickname) and Vera. It's no use staying here.'

We marched out in silence. Once outside they started talking nineteen to the dozen. They couldn't understand why, without asking me a single question, or even speaking to me, these doctors were so confident that I could not be trained to do anything.

'You know, Queen,' Mum said, 'young Gwen went to a training college and learnt to type, but she doesn't earn her living or do any work at home so maybe they think it is a waste of money to teach anyone else.'

'But, Bert, how do they know that everyone will be the same? Because Gwen doesn't go out to work it doesn't mean that Vera wouldn't do so if she were given the chance.'

'Aunt Queen,' I interrupted, 'Mrs. Collis has been trying for years to get me into a training college but nobody wants me— and I don't blame them,' I added, laughing.

'It would have been nice', Mum went on, 'for you to have been trained for something, but you are all right at home. I can always find you plenty to do.'

'Yes,' I thought to myself, 'but will it always be the same? Why did God make me as I am; surely it was to do something, but how can I help other people if first of all I'm not given a chance to prove what I can do myself.'

It was true I was happy at home now and Mum always told me I could do as I liked all day. This was very nice but I would have liked to have some work to do. I had been used to a responsible job at the unit, but now no one was dependent upon me; whereas, to a large extent, I was dependent upon others. Independence was the goal at which I aimed; a goal which seemed to come no nearer.

When the Ministry of Labour labelled me 'unemployable' they passed my papers back to the local authority who decided to send a home teacher twice a week. In due course a young lady arrived to teach me handcraft, and after some discussion we decided on basket-making with sea-grass. She showed me how to wind the grass on to a wooden frame and then weave it in and out. With a little practice I could make the baskets quite well, but the handles were much more difficult, because they had to be pulled very tight and held in that position while they were woven in. Much to my annoyance I found I could not master this part of the process and Mum had to make all the handles for me. I tried to explain to the young lady what the difficulty was, but she could not understand me very well, and as she was almost blind she could not see what I did wrong.

I thought it was rather a silly idea sending a blind person to teach someone with cerebral palsy. It was probably a good idea for the blind to teach the blind, but it made things very difficult for both of us when she could not understand what I was saying. After a time I found the sea-grass was making my hands very sore and, worse still, the manual effort required in basket-making brought back the pain in my wrist. I asked to be taught something different but the teacher always replied, 'As I can't see you very well I don't know what you're capable of doing.'

When she decided I was proficient in basket-making the teacher stopped calling and left me with a supply of sea-grass and instructions on what price to charge for the baskets when they were made. I carried on for a while but soon the pain in my wrist was so intense I was scared I would have to wear a sling again, so I gave up the work.

One of Mum's secret ambitions in life was to go abroad for a holiday and so, in 1952, she and Gladys arranged to go to Paris for a week if I could find someone to look after me during that time. They explained that they couldn't take me with them because I would find it very difficult to get up the gangway of a ship, and also, the trains in France were so high off the ground (or rather, the platforms were so low) it would be practically impossible for them to lift me into a train.

One day, when on a routine visit to the advice clinic, I told Mrs. Collis about Mum's hoped-for holiday and she immediately said, 'Why don't you come back to the unit for a week?'

Home

So it was arranged that in late September I should go to the unit for a week and Mum and Gladys should go to Paris.

I enjoyed my holiday at Queen Mary's, renewing old friendships and making new ones; playing with the children and watching them doing their work. It was a strange experience to come back as a visitor instead of as a member of the staff, and to see all my old jobs done by other people.

There were two teachers in the schoolroom and I smiled to myself when I saw this. 'That proves I did the work of a normal person,' I thought, 'people always told Judy there wasn't enough work for two women. I wonder if these two work as hard as we used to in the old days?'

The schoolroom now was in another part of the hospital instead of being in the unit, and the children were taken there each day. This was a good idea as it gave them a sense of going to school each day and made them feel more like their normal brothers and sisters.

Most of the children were aged between one and six years, and I was very surprised to notice that none of them wore skis. I was told that the reason for this was that the children were so young they had not got any bad habits to undo and therefore skis were unnecessary. It is true that while sitting at their tables most of the little ones looked quite normal—it was only when they started to walk or make any other difficult movement that one realized there was anything wrong with them.

In the evening I stood at the window looking at the distant hills, dreaming of days gone by. The hills faded from view and my life unfolded before me. I saw John as a little boy and then growing up. A smile broke across my face as I remembered the fun we had had together. My mind travelled on to the first morning Mrs. Collis had come to the unit—it had seemed like a dream, but a dream which I had never thought would materialize into this. I thought of all the staff that had trained here and had left, some of them to start cerebral-palsy units in other countries, and they were doing a good job of work. Last, but not least, I thought of the children. My dear children, what had become of them? From time to time I heard of a few of them, but what had become of the rest? Unfortunately many of the mothers had not understood how Mrs. Collis had trained their children while at the unit and had not properly grasped what she told them when, after years of hard work, she let them take their children home. She had always told them the truth about the best way to help their children, but very often the truth was not very pleasant to hear, and the mothers had taken their offspring elsewhere, mistakenly thinking that some different form of treatment could work a miraculous cure in them.

I sighed as I stood at the window watching the last red glow of the setting sun and thinking of a boy I had accidentally met a few weeks before. He had once been a patient in the unit and when he went home his mother took him to a hospital for a different kind of treatment. I asked him how he liked it, and he replied, 'Mum is always sorry she took me away from Mrs. Collis. I'm not getting on so well.'

The look on his face told the rest of the story.

'What a waste,' I said, thinking aloud, and then was brought quickly back to the present by an orderly calling me to supper.

At the end of the week Mrs. Collis asked if I would like to stay a little longer as she liked having me around. 'People don't normally like having me around,' I laughed, 'but I'd love to stay for a few more days.'

I wrote to Mum to ask her not to fetch me home for a little while and then a few days later, as I was walking from the treatment-room, I suddenly slipped and fell heavily with my feet underneath me. I had sprained a muscle in my ankle and had to be helped to bed where a cold compress was put on it. I couldn't stand for the next few days so most of the time was spent sitting in a wheel-chair in the nursery watching the children at play. On the day after the accident Mrs. Collis came towards me, smiling all over her face, and saying, 'I am sorry you've hurt your foot. We will have it X-rayed, but I don't think any bones are broken. Of course, now you'll have to stay here until you are better.'

Home

When the foot was beginning to get better I tried to walk into the nursery and found it very painful. As I hobbled along, leaning on the wall, one of the little children came towards me. His name was John, little John, and he had a very bad handicap, but he loved playing in his toy car—it was the only way he could get around. He pedalled up and said something which I could not understand very well. Kneeling beside him I inquired, 'What did you say, John? I did not quite hear you.'

'I said, let me help you.'

'But, John, how can you help me? I am a lot bigger than you.'

'I can help you,' he insisted. 'Lean on the bonnet of my car and I will take you to a chair. You will not hurt the car, Daddy sits on it sometimes.'

John was only six years of age and I had doubts about the wisdom of sitting on the car, but after his thoughtfulness I could not refuse. I sat gingerly down and held on carefully, but I needn't have been so nervous because John drove as carefully and slowly as if my life depended upon him.

Altogether I was at the unit for a month, during which time I did quite a lot of painting. One day, just for fun, I painted a picture of myself and gave it to Miss Kember, saying, 'You always wanted a picture of me.'

A few days later one of the teachers came up to me and said, 'You are a so-and-so. Because you painted yourself all the children are painting each other and I can't stop them. Jimmy painted Barbara's face green and told me that she looked like that when she'd eaten too many sweets!'

One of the new friends I made was Jane. She worked with Miss Kember in the nursery and it was not long before we found we had a lot in common. One morning she asked me to help her, and she told me about a friend of hers who had cerebral palsy. She said that he was very badly handicapped, and he lived in the Isle of Wight, and would I write to him because he did not have many friends. His name was Richard; and that was the beginning of another firm friendship.

Home

As Jane told me about Richard she sat on the edge of a small table at which we had been working. We had been laughing together but now, as she told the story of this young man, her expression turned to one of despair. Richard's father was a retired doctor, but the boy himself was so handicapped that he had to have a manservant to look after him. He had a brilliant mind and took a number of correspondence courses to improve his education. He could type with one finger and could instruct anyone on how to assemble a radio or television set.

Richard has the kind of handicap that makes his arms and legs shoot about uncontrollably. He feels quite helpless when he sits in a chair, because he has no control over his body, so he does all his work on the floor. Even all his electrical equipment is screwed to the floor.

Jane wondered if I could help him to overcome his handicap, but I found this practically impossible because he lived so far away, and, as he himself said, 'It took me thirty-five years to learn to do what I can do now, and I feel I am too old to be taught a new way of life now.'

So we correspond regularly and I welcome his letters, and occasionally we meet for a day together.

13

Camping with the Handicapped

Life seemed quiet at home after the month at the unit and I soon slid back into my old lazy routine. There was not much point in doing anything else. It made very little difference whether I rose at 7 or 9 a.m., the day was always long enough to do all that was necessary.

One day, in response to an inquiry by Mrs. Collis, the Ministry of Health invited me to go for an interview at their centre at King's Cross. There a doctor examined me to decide whether I was fit to be issued with a self-propelling chair and then passed me a catalogue, saying, 'Which of these chairs would you like?'

Eagerly I scanned the pages, but was disappointed to see none of these chairs had an engine. 'Please may I have a motor chair?' I asked. 'Some of my friends have got electric ones, and I am sure I could use one of those.'

The doctor shook her head.

'I am sorry. No one with paralysis is allowed to have a motor chair. You will have to have a hand-propelled one.'

I chose what appeared to be a suitable model and then went home. About a year later the chair was delivered, together with a large wooden shed in which to house it.

'At last', I thought, 'I shall be able to be a little independent and take myself out.' But alas, the chair was too large and heavy and no matter how I tried I could not move it. For several months I persevered but it was no use and Mum asked the

Ministry to change it for a smaller one. Within a few weeks the chair was exchanged for a junior model of a similar type, and once more I tried to take myself out. Gladys walked behind giving an occasional push, and everything was fine while we went along the level road, but directly we came to a hill I was defeated. Try as I might the chair would not go forward and Gladys had to push the whole time. I also had difficulty in turning corners. The chair was propelled forward by rotating two handles fixed to a chain attached to the front wheel by a long iron bar, and it was steered by moving the iron bar to either side. This meant that to turn a corner it was necessary to lean either to right or left and continue turning the handles. It was difficult enough to turn the handles when sitting up straight, but to try to do so while leaning to one side required much more strength in the wrists than I possessed.

After a great many attempts at learning to drive it became quite clear that I would never be able to go out alone in this chair. I had only to get to an awkward corner or a hill to be stranded, so reluctantly the chair was put away in its wooden shed and there, apart from an occasional outing with Gladys, it has remained ever since.

I still had my faithful old tricycle and Mum bought Gladys a second-hand bicycle so that we could go out cycling together. In the summer evenings and on Saturday afternoons we would ride through all the back streets where there was very little traffic. Occasionally we had to cross a main road and then Gladys would go across first and beckon me when the way was clear. On one occasion I was half-way across a very busy street when I heard the clang, clang, clang of a fire-engine close behind. Panic-stricken, I shot straight across the road past where Gladys was waiting, and up a side-street. Gladys was laughing fit to burst when she caught up. 'Oh, Vera, I have never seen you move so quickly before,' she chuckled. 'I thought you were in the London-to-Brighton race!'

I loved cycling, but dared not go out alone because my feet had to be strapped to the pedals and sometimes they slipped off.

Camping with the Handicapped

My feet would not stay on the pedals for long without straps and I could not fasten them myself. It had been all right while in Queen Mary's because I had never gone far from the unit and there was no traffic on the hospital roads, but on busy London streets it could have been dangerous to lose control and have no one there to help.

Cycling for pleasure was a wonderful pastime but I could not cycle too far or too quickly, so for long distances I had to rely on other people taking me by bus or train. One particular bus journey I have good cause to remember. It was soon after Christmas and Mum, Gladys and Aunt Queen were taking me to a party given by the Invalid Tricycle Association, of which I was a member. I had been given a pair of nylons as a present, my very first pair, and as Gladys helped me to put them on she uttered a warning to be careful not to catch them on anything.

The party was being held in a part of London with which we were unfamiliar, and Mum asked the conductor to tell us when we came to our stop. It was a Saturday afternoon an hundreds of people were doing their shopping when we stopped in a busy High Street and the conductor mumbled, 'Get off here.' The bus was running late and both conductor and driver were rather irritable.

A crowd of people jostled off the bus while we waited till last so as not to be in their way. Then Gladys and Aunt Queen took my arms to help me off. Gladys got off first, and I had one foot on the platform and one in the road when suddenly the bus started moving.

'Help!' screamed Mum. 'My daughters are being dragged along the road!'

'Stop the bus!' yelled Aunt Queen.

'Hang on!' shouted Gladys as, still clutching my arm, she was pulled along the road on her stomach.

A horrible minute passed. 'Will she be hurt?' I wondered. 'Will it kill her?' Eventually Aunt Queen let go of my other arm and I fell into the road on top of Gladys just as the bus pulled up.

Mum was still yelling at the conductor and now Aunt Queen

told the driver what she thought of him as a crowd of curious spectators left their Saturday afternoon shopping to see what all the fuss was about.

A kind gentleman helped me to my feet and then, thinking I was normal, let go and I immediately fell flat in the road again. Gladys picked herself up, took one look at the man's horrified expression, and burst out into peals of hysterical laughter. Mum and Aunt Queen were still arguing with the driver and conductor who were trying to gain the sympathy of the onlookers, and Gladys and I just sat in the road and laughed and laughed. Maybe it was shock, maybe it was relief to find that neither of us had anything worse than a few bruises, but suddenly the whole situation seemed incredibly funny.

Gladys explained to the kind gentleman, who was still looking aghast, that I had a handicap which made it difficult for me to stand, and I really hadn't hurt myself; and then we brushed the dust from our clothes and went on to our party. On arrival there we went into the cloakroom to wash some of the dirt off, and I looked at my knees and burst into tears.

'What's the matter, you are not really hurt, are you?' asked Gladys, as she searched for some hidden injury.

'My nylons, my lovely nylons,' I sobbed, as I looked at the tangled mass hanging around my legs. Both knees were grazed but I did not notice the blood, all I could see was the mass of broken and tattered threads where my beautiful stockings had been.

'Don't worry,' Gladys coaxed, as she bathed my knees. 'That is the first pair of nylons you have had and it will probably be the last for some time, but I will sue the bus company for the damage and then you can have something else with the money.' After a nice cup of tea we all felt much better, and I had control of myself again.

Her claim was met without argument for the cost of the stockings and repairs to her watch, which had been damaged in the fall, but it was some time before we had enough confidence to venture on a bus again.

Camping with the Handicapped

About this time a branch of a recently formed society called 'The Friends and Parents of Spastics', was opened in North London and we became active members. Once a month there was a social evening where we all joined in a sing-song and dance. It was good fun, though probably bad for our movement, to be able to 'let our hair down' amongst other handicapped people and their families and we all joined in the merriment as best we could. If any strangers had walked into the hall they would probably have had a shock to see our weird and jerky movements as we tried to dance, or to hear our croaky voices as we joined in a favourite song, but no one in the hall minded what anyone else looked like and we all had a jolly good time.

I wished that we could have them more often, for quite apart from letting myself go I really did enjoy watching and meeting other cerebral-palsied people.

But the time I looked forward to most of all was Sunday morning. Gladys and I joined a swimming club for handicapped people. If, like myself, one could not swim, there was always somebody to teach you how, but they went a long way around about it. I soon made friends with the man who ran the club and we had quite a lot of fun together. Sometimes I had to wait on the edge of the pool before I could go into the warm water, and it was always interesting to watch the people who could swim about in spite of their difficulties. But the morning used to go much too quickly and I would get dressed and return to my family. Although Gladys and I came and went from the pool together I did not see much of her while we were in the water. Mac (the leader) always asked her to help one of the many children who went there.

As I sat in the evenings making belts I would look forward to Sunday and all the fun we would have. Then I would look at Gladys sitting in the armchair knitting and I wished that I could do something like that, too.

Ever since I can remember people have told me I would never be able to knit, and I always believed them until one day Mum went shopping and came back with a very large pair of wooden needles. 'What are you going to make now, Mum?' I asked.

'I am not going to make anything,' she said with a smile. 'These are for you. I am going to teach you how to knit.'

'Oh well,' I thought, 'there is no harm in trying, but it will probably be a waste of time.'

After tea we sat side by side with a big ball of carpet wool and these outsize needles.

'You can start by making a knitted slip mat and see how you get on,' Mum said, as she cast on a number of stitches. She knitted the first few rows and then gave it to me.

'Please don't watch me, Mum, it puts me off,' I pleaded. 'Let me do it in my own way.' After a few minutes I made my first stitch and to say I was surprised is putting it mildly. I had taken much more than a stitch. I had proved to everyone, including myself, that everyone had been wrong, and I realized that I did not know what I could do until I tried. The joy of achievement gained with that first stitch remained with me for days.

Gradually I progressed to knitting on smaller needles and with finer wool, and was immensely proud the day I finished making my first bed-jacket. Since then I have made a number of articles, but knitting is not one of my favourite hobbies, because, for me, it is too slow and monotonous.

The days at home passed uneventfully until holiday time came around once again. I had joined a society called 'The Spastic Fellowship' who had their headquarters at Liverpool, and when the society decided to spend a get-together week at a holiday camp in Blackpool, we took advantage of the opportunity to go along.

About thirty of us arrived at the camp. Approximately half of this number were cerebral-palsied children and young adults and the other half were their mothers. The people at the holiday camp could not have been nicer. They went out of their way to make our holiday a success, and instead of the pitying look we usually receive in strange places we were given a bright smile and a helping hand from staff and holiday-makers alike. Of course there were a few holiday-makers who objected to our presence, and who were typified by the one who complained to the management, saying, 'It is most upsetting to have to keep coming in contact with such unsightly people as these. You should not have allowed them to come here.'

But this attitude made no difference to the manager, who told them bluntly, 'If you don't like looking at them, then look the other way. These people need a holiday just as much as you do, in fact more so, and we are trying to give them a good time.'

The holiday camp was near an airfield, and one day the whole of the Spastic Fellowship decided to go for a ten-shilling joy-ride. We piled into two aeroplanes, that is all except one mother who was rather nervous and preferred to stay on the ground. 'I'll hold your handbags and then I'll be rich if you don't come back,' she joked, as we left her surrounded by our belongings.

The first plane took off and then ours, a smaller one, circled the aerodrome. Every two seconds someone would say, 'We are off, no we're not'; 'Now we are in the air. No we are not, we are still on the ground!' The pilot circled the field twice and then taxied back to the hangar.

'You have a screw loose,' yelled a mechanic, as he ran out with a spanner. 'Just a jiffy, and I'll fix it.'

The screw fixed, once more we circled the field, and this time rose gracefully into the air and out over the sea. As we turned to go back towards Blackpool Tower I saw the tip of the wing, through the window, and my stomach seemed to come up to my mouth. But the feeling didn't last. I was too excited by this new experience to be worried for long.

'Look down there,' called Gladys, 'that must be a cemetery.'

'Isn't it odd to see all those different coloured tombstones,' added Mum.

'Tombstones nothing,' came a voice from someone who had been on the flight before. 'That is a caravan site!'

After a very happy week at the holiday camp Friday came all too soon, and with it the fancy dress parade.

'What are you going as?' asked Mrs. A., the mother of one of the children in our party.

'Oh, I am not going in it, I have nothing to wear.'

'Well, I have a kimono in my chalet; I wear it as a dressing-gown, but if you would like to borrow it you could dress up as a Japanese lady.'

'Oh, good!' I replied enthusiastically. 'I will go as Madame Butterfly.' Gladys made paper flowers for my hair, a paper fan to carry, and rosettes to decorate the wheels of my invalid chair, and fully dressed in the kimono I was taken into the dance-hall.

There were quite a large number of entries for the fancy dress parade, including about six of our party, who had dressed themselves up as a wedding group and went in under the title 'The Bride Wore Boots'. They looked so funny as they wobbled down the dance-hall, all looking slightly drunk, and with the 'bride' holding up her long white dress to show her surgical boots. The onlookers were not quite sure whether to laugh or cry at first, so they applauded and said what a good effort it was.

Soon it was my turn to parade and I felt rather silly and shy as Gladys pushed me round the hall. I held the fan in front of my face and peeped coyly over the top and everyone thought it was part of the act. We came to the end of the hall and stood in line with the other competitors waiting for the judges' decision. Next to me was a large man dressed as an Indian prince.

'If you win, I'll kiss you,' he laughed.

'All right, and I'll do the same if you win.'

The announcer called through the microphone: 'First, the Indian prince. Will his Royal Highness kindly step this way?' So the Indian Prince went up to the stage and the band played 'Indian Summer'.

'Second, Madame Butterfly.' There was a spontaneous burst

of applause as the band struck up 'One Fine Day', and thrilled to bits I went forward to receive my prize.

'What do we do now?' joked the Indian prince. 'We have both won. Do we kiss each other?'

'Why not?' I laughed, as he gave me a congratulatory hug.

Now, whenever I hear the tune 'One Fine Day', vivid memories of that happy evening come flooding back.

Back at home the children in the flats were becoming increasingly noisy and rude. A number of them now had got into the habit of standing outside our french windows and staring in while we were having meals. Tennis balls were thrown through the bedroom and kitchen windows and when we refused to return these to their mischievous owners irate parents came down and demanded them.

The nervous tension which this produced, coupled with the fact that I was not now getting sufficient fresh air, helped to make me anaemic and I started to lose weight. My normal weight is $7\frac{1}{2}$ stone, but in a short time this was down to less than 6 stone and I felt I had no energy to do anything. The local doctor called every week for months and prescribed iron pills and milk foods which stopped me from getting worse, but did not noticeably improve my health. Eventually Mum decided that the only answer to the problem was to move away from the flat and get a house in the country. We could not afford to buy a house so we asked the L.C.C. to transfer us to one of their out-of-London estates.

The time was May 1953, and at the end of the month we all went to Blackpool once again to see if ten days by the sea would help to calm our nerves. We stayed at the same holiday camp as before and the staff remembered us and gave us a great welcome.

We enjoyed the holiday, but somehow it was not quite the same as it had been the year before, because we missed the happy companionship of the other members of the fellowship. During the week-end a number of people afflicted with polio, which is quite different from cerebral palsy, came to the camp, together with the Red Cross nurses who were looking after them, and with them we went for a day's coach ride to the Lake District. No one who wanted to go on the trip was left behind, even one young girl who lay flat on her back on a stretcher was taken. The seats in the coach were rearranged to allow for the stretcher and wheel-chairs to be accommodated. Many of these people had spent months in hospital beds, or at home surrounded by four brick walls, and they revelled in the early summer sunshine, as they gazed enraptured at the majestic beauty of the hills and lakes which we passed on our journey.

Our holiday over we lived only for the day when we could move into our house in the country, and eagerly we watched every post in the hope that the transfer would not be long delayed. June came and went and now it was July, and soon it would be time for me to go camping with the Rangers again. Then, one morning, the long-awaited letter arrived asking Mum to go on the following Tuesday to view a new three-roomed house at Merstham in Surrey.

Of course we were all delighted and the whole week-end we talked of nothing else but what the house would be like. There were difficulties to be faced. For one thing the rent was higher and then expenses would be greater because there were no markets near Merstham for cheap shopping. It would also mean that I would have to give up my swimming club and Gladys would have to travel about three hours each day to get to and from her job in London, and her fares would cost about an extra £1 a week. Even so we considered these sacrifices worth while if we could have a little peace and quiet and could enjoy the privacy of a small garden.

At last Tuesday came and Mum, Gladys and Aunt Queen set out for Merstham, leaving me with a plate of sandwiches, a bottle of milk complete with drinking straw, and the promise that they would be back early in the afternoon.

While they were gone I could not concentrate on anything. My thoughts ran round in circles. 'Will they take the house? Will it be suitable? How will I get upstairs? I have never walked upstairs by myself. What will the garden be like, and will I be able to sit out there?'

The minutes seemed like hours. Would the time never pass? I kept looking at the clock and wishing it would go faster so that I would know the answers to my questions. At 3 o'clock I heard Mum's key turn in the lock and I felt my heart thumping hard. The rhythm of its beats seemed to say over and over again, 'Have they taken the house? Have they taken it?' I felt sick with excitement as Gladys walked into the room.

'Well?' My eyes finished the question.

Gladys was smiling and I knew the answer before she spoke, 'Oh, yes, we have taken the house and we are to move there in a fortnight's time.'

For the next two weeks we were very busy packing and throwing out all the useless things that somehow accumulate in cupboards. At the same time I was preparing to go to camp; uniform, underwear and bed linen all had to be marked with my name and pressed and packed. The removal was planned for Monday and I was due to go to camp the following day, so Aunt Queen invited me to stay with her for a couple of days so that I would not be in the way at home. It meant that I would go straight to camp from her flat and would not see our new home until I returned a fortnight later, but arrangements for my transport to camp had all been made from London and this seemed the best plan.

Aunt Queen lived in a large ground-floor flat with all the rooms leading off on each side from a long passage. It often reminded me of a ship with cabins on either side. The bedrooms were at one end of the corridor and at the other was the office where Aunt Queen's husband, Uncle Len, worked all day.

Aunt Queen took me home with her on Sunday evening and the following morning she brought me a cup of tea in bed, and said, 'Good morning, Vera, I am just going up to see your Mum in case she needs any help this morning. I will give you your breakfast in bed and you can get up when you like. If you want any help just call Uncle Len, he is in his office.'

Directly I heard the front door close behind her I slid out of bed and went into the bathroom to wash and dress. Having tidied up I started walking slowly and carefully along the passage towards the sitting-room, just as Uncle Len came out of his office.

'Hullo there, Vera. I am just coming to comb your hair and do up your boots. Why didn't you call me if you are ready?' He stopped suddenly with a look of surprise on his face. 'Oh, I see you don't need any help, you have managed by yourself.'

'I always manage by myself,' I answered a little smugly, and added, with a grin, 'Did you think I needed waiting on?'

The sequel to this incident was that a few months later, when another of Mum's sisters was visiting London, she told me one day, 'Aunt Queen could not get over how much you do for yourself. She always thought you needed a lot of help. If you ever want a holiday you can always come and stay with me.'

'By myself?'

'Of course, you don't need your Mum to look after you.'

This was quite an announcement because this particular aunt had a bad leg which she had to be very careful of, and I never dreamt that she would take the risk of having me around her house.

Aunt Queen came back with the news that everything had gone according to plan and Mum and Gladys were well on their way to Merstham and our new home. For a while I sat and tried to picture what the new house would be like, but soon the excitement of going to camp the following day put all other thoughts out of my head.

I have been to camp many times since leaving the women's hospital, and have enjoyed them all, but I well remember the first occasion when I didn't want to go at all. Somehow I thought that camping with a lot of handicapped girls would be rather like living in hospital, and I was never more surprised in my life than on that first trip to 'Woodlarks'.

I felt very miserable in my new navy-blue uniform, sitting in a wheel-chair at Waterloo Station, amongst all the strange

faces. There were about forty girls and women on the platform
waiting for the train. They were all dressed alike, and all seemed
to know each other very well as they laughed and talked. About
half of them were handicapped in various ways and the other
half were normal girls who were going along as our helpers.
The train came in to the platform, and everyone helped everyone else, and soon we were all on our way to 'Woodlarks' at
Farnham in Surrey.

There are many camp sites in England for Scouts and Guides,
but this one is unique because it was built specially for handicapped people. It is situated in lovely wooded grounds, with
no steps to any of the buildings, and the camp chapel is an
open-air site in the centre of a ring of tall pine trees. The camp
swimming-pool was built largely by voluntary labour and is
secluded by trees and bushes so that it is warm there even in
cool weather. A ramp into the shallow end of the pool allows
an old basket chair to be taken right down into the water,
and hand-rails on either side of the ramp help to support those
campers who cannot use their legs. In this way practically
everyone can make use of the pool.

All the helpers and those handicapped campers who have
permission from their doctors sleep in tents; the rest sleep in a
large brick building with toilet facilities built along one side.
Meals are mostly cooked and eaten in the open air, but if the
weather happens to be bad then there is another brick hut
which is used for this purpose.

On arrival at camp everyone is put into a patrol. Usually there
are about ten girls in each patrol, five normal ones and five
handicapped. A handicapped girl is chosen as leader and it is
her job to allocate the daily chores to the members of her patrol.
Every girl is given some job no matter how small, or how bad
her handicap, and the whole camp is thrown out of balance if
she fails to do that job.

Immediately after breakfast and before the daily work is begun we all assemble for colour parade. The Union Jack is
hoisted by the patrol whose duty it is for that day, and this is

followed by a short prayer and hymn. Dinner is prepared and the camp tidied, and then often a senior Guide or a visitor gives a talk on Guiding. By the time this is finished we have all developed hearty appetites which are more than satisfied by the delicious meals prepared by the cooking patrol on an open-air fire. Most afternoons are spent in or by the swimming-pool and the day ends with a camp-fire singsong.

Usually there are some unrehearsed fun and games and it often takes the poor helpers a couple of hours to get everyone to bed. One evening when I eventually went into my tent, sat on the pillow and pushed my feet under the bedclothes, I accidentally toppled over and turned a backwards somersault. My feet slipped under the edge of the tent and I found myself on my knees in the field.

Mrs. Gentry, who was camp commandant, happened to be passing. 'I thought I told you to go to bed,' she said, with mock severity, 'and here you are sitting in the middle of a field at 10 o'clock at night, wearing nothing but your pyjamas!'

'I am sorry,' I apologized between giggles, 'but you know my bed isn't big enough.'

On one day in every camp, patrols have their dinner in the woods. The girls who cannot walk are pushed there in their wheel-chairs and carry the food on their laps until they reach a small clearing. Then all the food is hung in net bags from trees until it is required and everyone sets about the job of lighting a fire. Twigs and dried leaves are gathered and small logs are added as the fire blazes. No cooking utensils are taken on this trip. All the food, which usually consists of sausages, potatoes and flour, has to be cooked with nature's aids only. The potatoes are baked in their jackets in the ashes of the fire and the sausages are stuck on to the end of peeled sticks and held over the heat. More often than not 'dampers' are served for pudding. These are simply small rounds of dough, made out of flour and water, mixed in a billy-can, and roasted on the end of sticks in the same way as the sausages. They are eaten hot with jam or butter.

Camping with the Handicapped

As a Ranger I have had so much fun at camp that I have often asked other girls who have not been on one of these holidays, 'Why don't you go to camp this year? Not everyone who camps is a Guide or Ranger, but of course you can take a bigger and more interesting part if you are.' The answer is nearly always the same. 'I am much too handicapped to go. I cannot even dress myself, and I could not pass any of the Ranger tests.' I explain that there are always plenty of helpers, and even if a girl is flat on her back on a stretcher there is no reason why she should not enjoy a camping holiday. As for passing tests I tell them of my own experience when attempting the pre-enrolment test of taking a friend out for a day.

It was Mrs. Gentry's first year at an extension camp, and she had come as a helper, so I asked her to accompany me. I thought that if I took the divisional commissioner nothing could go wrong, and I would pass the test easily. At about 11 a.m. we collected our sandwich lunch from the cookhouse, and with me seated in my wheel-chair, on top of a pile of groundsheets, we set out.

We were going to a place called Frenches Pond and I studied the map carefully. The first mile or so was along a straight road, so there was no chance of going wrong, but soon we came to a village green with three roads leading from it. Which was the correct one? There were no signposts. The camp nurse had told us to go one way but the map seemed to direct us in the opposite way, so Mrs. Gentry said, 'Let's go the way the nurse told us. The map might be out of date.'

She pushed me up a steep hill at the top of which was a lovely cornfield. We decided this was a good place to stop for lunch and sat ourselves down on the groundsheets, just inside the gate. It was the highest hill for miles around and the view was magnificent. Clouds passed across the sun and we watched the rain falling on distant hills. Soon it reached us and it seemed as if the heavens opened. We had no mackintoshes with us, so we covered ourselves with the groundsheets, leaving only our eyes showing. Several people passed along the road and eyed us in amazement. They seemed unable to decide whether we were outsize molehills or some new type of monster.

The storm ended as suddenly as it had begun and we crawled from our rubber tents, dry as a bone. Mrs. Gentry fetched the old wheel-chair from its hiding-place under the hedge and as we folded up our groundsheets she casually remarked, 'Do you know, Vera, I think we have gone wrong somewhere.'

The thought had struck me, too, so I agreed with her sugges- tion that we should go down the hill again and follow the map. We went down much more quickly than we had come up, and on the way Mrs. Gentry paused to let us have a last long look at the view. 'I am glad we took the wrong turning, Vera. That was a lovely place to have our lunch and we would never have found it if we had followed the map correctly.'

'How right you are,' I agreed, 'it is a good thing to get away from everyone sometimes and to be at peace with the world for a little while.'

From the bottom of the hill we followed the map along the road for about a mile and then turned off into a small path. The path started at the end of some private gardens and gradually led us along the side of a steep hill which was covered with trees and shrubs. At first it was a smooth wide path, but as we went farther it narrowed and became rough and bumpy until it was just a grass slope leading up to some back gardens.

Mrs. Gentry stopped for breath and gasped, 'I don't like this path much. I cannot help the chair shaking so badly.' Then, after a pause, she added, 'I do hope you will not fall out.'

'I never fall out,' I boasted. Hardly had the words left my lips than the chair went over an extra large stone and tipped up, and I fell on to the grass. I just could not do anything for laugh- ing, but lay on the grass and roared and roared. When Mrs. Gentry realized I was not hurt she joined in, and I am sure the noise we made must have been heard for miles around.

We had now realized that this was not the right way either, so we went back to the road, but we were not to find Frenches Pond that day because when we reached the main road we found the camp nurse driving along in her car, looking for the happy wanderers. She took us back to camp and later that day I was enrolled as a Ranger, by Mrs. Gentry, because I had passed my test! I had not done what I set out to do, but I had made the most of what came along, and that is what Guiding is for; to teach girls to make the most of their opportunities. Mrs. Gentry and I always agree that we achieved more that day than we would have done if we had reached our objective. For a short time we had been close to God and had seen the wonders of His work in nature, undistracted by man or machine.

Quite a number of girls who go to camp have cerebral palsy, and secretly I always try to diagnose and help them. It is fatal to say, 'What is wrong with you?' because the answer is usually, 'I am a spastic.' They do not realize that this is simply one of the types of cerebral palsy, and more likely they are afflicted with quite a different form.

Priss was one girl I particularly longed to help, but I was unable to do so. It was a Saturday afternoon, our first day in camp, when I asked the Ranger with the teapot to pour me another cup of tea.

'Not unless you help me with the washing-up,' she joked. She knew that she was safe in making this suggestion, because all our 'crockery' at camp is unbreakable.

While we were in the cookhouse Priss's father came in his car to bring something which his daughter had forgotten. Priss had cerebral palsy of a very severe type. She was wild in her movements and flung her arms and legs in all directions. Because of this no one would sit near her, and not many people could understand what she was saying because her speech was so bad. Above all she was very handicapped emotionally. Immediately she saw her father she began to kick and scream, 'I want to go home, I want to go home!'

Her poor father felt he could do nothing but take her home, and as they passed the cookhouse she was still crying. The girl who was washing-up with me said sadly, 'Poor Priss, I thought she was happy here.'

'She was, but she is like a lot of people who have not learned to behave well in society. What her father should have done is to have left her alone for a while.'

'You seem to know a lot about her, Vera.'

'I do. I was something like her once.'

At that moment a number of girls came into the room and my thoughts went back to the time when I first met Mrs. Collis. I remembered the number of times she had put me in the bathroom to cool down and learn that society will not tolerate spoilt behaviour, and as I washed a rubber cup I wondered how long it would be before I could tell the world my story and how much more I would have to learn about life before I could put it on paper.

14

Holiday in France

CRSSSSD

At camp I always have a good time and never want to go home, but this year it was different. We had been camping at the beautiful Roman site at Dudsbury, near Bournemouth, and, as usual, I had enjoyed myself very much, but I was anxious to get home to see our new house.

'I wonder what the new house will be like? Will I be able to walk upstairs? Mum said there is no W.C. downstairs so I shall have to get up there somehow. I have never walked upstairs in my life except with a great deal of help from other people; how am I going to manage now? How big is the garden and shall I be able to help with it?' These thoughts and many others kept running through my head. I had counted the days to camp and now impatiently I counted them until it was time to go home again. On the last night there I was much too excited to sleep and was very glad that we had to rise early the next morning in order to clear up before leaving.

When everything was packed and the tents dismantled we sat with the luggage waiting for the coach. The other girls were all talking about what a lovely camp it had been but I sat quietly, not hearing their conversation, thinking only that I would be sleeping in my own bed in our new house that night.

Our journey home took us through some of England's most picturesque scenery. We passed through the New Forest with its wild ponies, across the Hog's Back and around the perimeter of the Devil's Punchbowl. The country-side lay before us like a patchwork quilt and the glorious colours of the gorse and shrubland with its purple and red hues seemed too brilliant to be real. It looked as if a giant had stretched an enormous canvas before him and had then used every colour in his palette.

Soon we reached North London and one of the active Rangers helped me from the coach, across the road to Aunt Queen's flat. There Mum was waiting, and Gladys arrived soon after she had finished work. Mum and Aunt Queen had not seen each other for a fortnight so naturally they had a lot to talk about, and anxiously I watched the clock, wishing that we could go home. Eventually, we left and made our way by bus to Victoria Station where we caught the train to Merstham. Our house is a good fifteen minutes' walk from the station, and it seemed that we would never get there. By now it was dark, and I realized that ironically I would not really be able to see the house until the next day. As we passed through the wide new roads, with the little cottages on either side, it seemed that we were walking through fairyland as lights twinkled from all the windows.

It was about 9 p.m. when Mum turned the key in our front door and my heart missed a beat. Butterflies chased each other around my tummy as we went inside. We were in a small hall and there were the stairs, the obstacle which had to be overcome. Turning my back on them for the moment I investigated the ground floor and was delighted to see that a comfortable living-room led into a large well-equipped kitchenette. The garden would have to wait until the morning but, so far, there were no difficulties. There were no awkward corners and the doors were large.

Now the question had to be faced. How was I going to get upstairs? It had to be done somehow. My bedroom and the bathroom were up there; I was too heavy to be carried, so we all stood at the bottom of the stairs thinking.

Mum spoke. 'You have got to get up there somehow, show me how you are going to do it.'

'Hold on to the handrail, and I will walk behind you,' suggested Gladys.

'No, I don't think I will walk up them, I might fall and hurt myself. It would be better to sit on the bottom stair and while holding on to the handrail lift my seat up one step at a time.'

There were fourteen stairs and it took about five minutes to reach the top going up them in this way on my seat, but it could be done, that was the important point. For about three months I continued going up and down stairs in this way until the day when Mum came home with some coco-nut matting stair carpet.

'This is good hard-wearing stuff,' Mum said, as she fixed it to the stairs. 'It should last for years.'

She was right, but oh my poor bottom when I had gone up and down the stairs a few times. It felt as though I had been sitting on sandpaper! It was obvious that I would have to use my feet instead of my seat or all my pocket-money would be spent on underwear.

When Gladys came home I followed her upstairs and surprised her by saying, 'I want to walk down. Will you please walk in front so that I will have something soft to fall on if necessary?'

We went down together. This time I stood up and held on tightly to the hand-rail. It was not so difficult as I had imagined. I had only to overcome the giddiness which I felt when looking down the stairs and to stifle the fear of falling from top to bottom. We practised going up and down for some time and very soon I was able to tackle the stairs alone. Another obstacle had been surmounted. True I held the hand-rail with both hands and hung on rather tightly—so tightly in fact that on two occasions the rail came right out from the wall and had to be re-fixed—but as time went on I found the stairs were no longer the terrifying barrier they once had been, and eventually I found I could ascend and descend those fourteen steps in about a minute. Now I can even go up and down those stairs quickly enough to get change for anyone waiting at the front door, and it always makes Mum laugh when I say, 'I am just going to run upstairs.'

It was wonderful living in the country with our own little garden and the open fields and farmland only a few minutes' walk from home. It was peaceful after the hustle and bustle of life in a flat in London, and soon we all became more relaxed and happy. As is often the way on a new estate people were glad to get to know each other and pass the time of day, and soon we found we knew so many people we could not go the length of the street without stopping for a chat. Various clubs were formed and we were welcomed into a number of these. The only thing I missed was the Sunday morning swimming club and we now lived rather a long distance from a swimming-pool.

Time was passing, Christmas came and went, and then one cold January day in 1954 Mrs. Collis came to see me. She told me about a cerebral-palsied boy in Ireland who had written his autobiography, and asked why I had never fulfilled the promise I had made to her many years before. With her encouragement I started once again to write my life story, using as a guide the notes made previously. It was difficult but interesting and I spent four or five hours every day working at the typewriter.

Soon after Mrs. Collis's visit Mrs. Gentry came to tea and asked if I would like to go on a trip to France. In June a party of Rangers from Essex were going to St. Malo and they had a vacancy which I could fill. At first I did'nt believe her. How could I go abroad? I had never even dreamed of it as I thought I was much too handicapped to get on or off a ship. However, she reassured me that the offer was genuine, and I gladly accepted.

Mrs. Gentry also asked if I would like to become a post captain in the Girl Guides. It would mean that I would have to take a course which every captain has to take whether or not she is handicapped, the only difference being that I would have to send my test papers through the post. I explained to Mrs. Gentry that I would gladly take the course but because of my

scanty education I was rather dubious about the result. However, when the first test papers were returned after marking I
was surprised and overjoyed to find that the examiner had given
high marks. True it was only a simple test, but at twenty-six
years of age it was the first examination paper I had ever completed, and I felt I was really learning something at last.

The next three months passed very quickly and every day
was spent in typing the book or working on the Girl Guide
course. In early April a new difficulty arose. Every time I
started to type my eyes began to hurt and my nose ran as
though I had hay fever. I thought it was just a cold but it got
no better, so for about a month I did nothing but sit in the
garden painting pictures. It was the only thing I could do without discomfort; knitting, sewing, reading and writing all
brought on the agonizing pain around my eyes. After a while
my nose became swollen and sore and breathing through it was
difficult. Mum sent for the doctor, who prescribed nose-drops,
and for a time these alleviated the trouble.

It was now June and time to go to France. Even when all
the formalities for obtaining passport, currency, etc., were
completed I could not really believe that I would ever get there.
At night I dreamt about the trip and more than once awoke in a
cold sweat after a nightmare that the ship had sunk in the middle
of the Channel and we were all drowning. At last the long-
awaited day came.

It was a beautifully sunny morning as Mum and Gladys took
me on the train to Girl Guide Headquarters in London. Mrs.
Nichols, the divisional commissioner for London, and Miss
Simmons, the captain of the Essex Post Rangers, were there to
meet us, and together with five other handicapped Rangers I
left by car for Southampton. A Guider, who was accompanying
us on the trip as a helper, was in charge of all the people who
were going to Southampton by train and all the luggage. She
left headquarters in a taxi for Waterloo Station, surrounded by
haversacks, suitcases, walking-sticks and crutches. In fact, there
was so much luggage that the obliging taxi driver asked her to

get in the cab first so that he could arrange it around her. It must have been a strange sight when she arrived at the station complete with enough crutches to equip a small hospital and we often wondered what the puzzled bystanders thought.

When the main party arrived at the docks the St. John's Ambulance Brigade were ready, as usual, to give their assistance with the luggage and chair cases. Our small party had arrived by car some two hours previously and had been allowed to go on board straight away.

I had often been told that I would never be able to go abroad because I would not be able to get up the gangway of a ship and yet here I was, walking up on my own. I had a handrail on each side to grasp and Mrs. Nichols was walking behind, but nevertheless I was walking, walking, up and up. I wanted to shout, 'Look, everybody, I am walking on to a ship!'

Of course I did not say anything, but smiling broadly, reached the deck and sat down next to my friend Edith, who is very badly handicapped with cerebral palsy.

Shortly before 9 p.m., when everyone was aboard, the gangway was removed and we slid out of the harbour and away to the strange land across the sea. As the white cliffs of Dover receded into the distance I felt a sudden twinge of sadness at the thought of leaving England. This feeling soon disappeared as the leaders of our party began introducing everyone to everyone else and we all talked incessantly of the wonders which lay in store.

There were twelve handicapped girls in our party and it was not long before we were taken to our first-class cabins, three girls to each cabin. This came as quite a surprise as I had expected to sleep in a chair in the lounge, and the luxury of the cabin was quite overwhelming. Actually I do not think we had paid for cabins but the captain of the ship had taken pity on us and insisted that we should have every comfort.

Several stewards looked in to see if we required any help and showed us the bell to ring if we needed anything. They assured us that the crossing would be calm and we would not be ill.

Their forecast was correct; the small ship rocked only enough to send me to sleep, and I knew no more until the following morning when one of the helpers shook my arm.

'Come on, Vera, it is 5.30 a.m., and we dock at 7.'

She helped me to wash and dress as the confined space in the cabin and the excitement made it difficult for me to manage alone.

When all the other travellers had left the ship our party of thirty Rangers and Guiders walked or were carried by French porters on to French soil. The two cars in which six of us had travelled to Southampton had been brought to France as well and were taken off the ship by crane. As they were hoisted far above our heads, Mrs. Nichols said, 'Good gracious, I have never seen the bottom of my car before. Doesn't it look odd.'

Most of the party climbed into a waiting coach and the rest of us took our places once more in the cars. We did not talk on the way to our destination, as Mrs. Nichols did not know the road and had to follow the coach in front, with the added difficulty of driving on the 'wrong' side of the road. Sitting there I began to feel rather hungry. We had had only a cup of tea that morning as we were going to have breakfast at our journey's end. I was dreaming of a nice big meal. 'I hope they don't give me too much, I am not a big eater,' I thought, 'but I am hungry!'

Soon we turned down a side street and passed through a pair of huge grey iron gates. At the end of an avenue of trees stood the Convent of St. Anne, a forbidding-looking building, which was to be our home for the next ten days.

The coach was already being unloaded as we pulled up, and a nun came across the gravel drive to shake hands with Mrs. Nichols. 'I am Sister Gabriel and I am the only nun who speaks any English.' she explained. 'I hope you and your handicapped girls will have a restful holiday. Have they been out of hospital long?'

'My handicapped girls', replied Mrs. Nichols kindly, 'are not ill, and we have come over here to have a good time.'

'Do exactly as you like,' Sister Gabriel answered with a smile. 'The Mother Superior told me to tell you not to be quiet on our account. Now I expect you want your breakfast, so come with me.'

'Food at last,' we all murmured, as we followed her into the large dining-hall. Then everyone's face fell. Mouths dropped open in horror as we saw the tables set for our party, and neatly arranged at each place was one crusty roll and one knob of butter! Perhaps French people could manage on such a tiny breakfast, but it seemed like starvation diet to us with the enormous appetites we had gained from our channel crossing. It was even worse for a couple of the girls who, because of their handicap, found it practically impossible to eat anything so hard as a crusty roll, and so they had no breakfast at all.

I looked at the small bowl set next to my plate. 'If this is a finger-bowl I shall not be able to wash my hands in it,' I said dismally.

'Don't be silly,' laughed one of the girls, 'that's your coffee-cup!'

Breakfast over, we were taken upstairs to the dormitory where we were to sleep, and after we had unpacked we had a rest on our beds. I managed to get up the stairs without help, but a number of the girls had to be carried and one even had to be carried in her wheel-chair. Usually it took six Rangers pushing and pulling together to get her up the two flights of stairs, as she was no light weight, so after that first day we made sure we never went upstairs unless it was time to go to bed.

The convent had been founded as a school, but because of the war and money difficulties it had been turned into a hotel convent for French gentlefolk. It could hold about one hundred people but there were only sixty guests while we were there. The only time we saw the other residents was at meals and then they eyed us rather as some queer species. They could not understand our habit of standing or sitting bolt upright before each meal and singing grace.

One night I sat in the dining-hall after supper, waiting for

someone to walk with me upstairs. I did not want to go up
alone in case I met any of the other guests who could not speak
English, and who might have been worried if they had seen me
fall. One of the little French maids was clearing the table and
she tried to speak to me but her English was about as good as
my French, so we had to manage as best we could with sign
language. We learned quite a lot about each other in this way,
it is surprising how much it is possible to find out about a
person by simply using signs, and I was quite sorry when
someone came to take me to bed.

Each day when the weather was fine we went down to the
beach or for a walk through the small fishing town. Most of the
houses had been shattered by bombs during the war and were
in quite a bad state of repair. The people seemed poor and were
old-fashioned in their dress, and everything smelled of fish or
decaying property. It was a depressing town and made me feel
thankful for the considerably higher standard of living which
we enjoy in England and which we do not always appreciate.

Quite early in our holiday the whole party, thirty of us, went
to the bank to change our travellers' cheques. The poor bank
clerk didn't know who to serve first, there were so many of us,
so we were told to stand in line against the wall of the bank,
both inside and out, and then he served us one at a time. It was
all rather funny, but I did feel grand sitting in a bank and sign-
ing my own cheques.

As soon as we had some money in our pockets we enjoyed
ourselves by going to the little market, which sprawled through
a few narrow streets, to buy souvenirs. Only four girls in our
party could speak any French and very few of the stallholders
knew more than a couple of words of English, as we were staying in a part of the town unfrequented by English tourists, so
it took anything up to half an hour to make one small purchase.
First we asked the price and then translated this into English
and worked out the equivalent in British money, and then probably decided it was too dear and started the whole process over
again with another article. None of us had a great deal of

money to spend, so the presents we bought were usually valued
at no more than a few shillings, and the small margin of profit
the stallholder made was well earned by the time he had made a
sale.

The market itself fascinated me. It was gayer than any I had
seen in England and there were so many stalls squeezed on to
such a tiny piece of ground. It was the first time I had seen a real
market square and the place had a magic all its own. Perhaps it was
the cobbled streets, or the brightly coloured covered stalls that
sold everything except food (which was sold in another part of
the town); maybe it was the fact that some of the market streets
led to the sea, but whatever it was it seemed like going into
another world, a world of noise and colour.

After our trips to the town we would return to the convent
and sit in the cloisters to show each other our purchases, but
unfortunately the weather was not very kind, so we asked for a
room which we could use for morning prayers and to sit in on
wet days. The room which we were given was large and dark
and had about five doors leading into the cloisters and various
rooms inside the building. The wooden floor was highly
polished and the furniture was fragile antique which we were
afraid to touch in case it fell apart. Most of it was badly worm-
eaten and the girls with wooden crutches took care not to leave
them against the furniture in case the wood worm crawled into
them, too. The whole room seemed to smell of decay. One girl
was so afraid of the place that in no circumstances would she
go in there. She felt that it was haunted and even in the wettest
weather she preferred to sit in the cold damp cloisters, probably
reading a murder story, rather than take the chance, as she
thought, of seeing a ghost.

Often in the afternoon when it was raining we stayed in this
room and played cards, and when anyone unexpectedly came in
we pushed the cards quickly under the table and just sat there
like a lot of stuffed dummies. On one occasion Sister Gabriel
put her head round the door and remarked, 'You are quiet.
Do please make a noise. You are on holiday, not a lot of nuns!'

Whenever she came in after that we sang a camp-fire song to her, and this seemed to convince her that we were having a good time.

One morning one of the Guiders took me for a walk to the beach and as we sat there with our backs against the sea wall we talked of many things. She told me that she earned her living as a hospital car driver and that although she had never met Mrs. Collis, she knew quite a lot about her from the people she drove to and from the hospital. On the way back to the convent the Guider bought a bottle of wine so that at dinner we could drink a toast to Mrs. Collis and her work.

The wine was not very intoxicating, but it caused a lot of comment from the other girls who teased us unmercifully; and that evening, as I walked upstairs with Sheila, one of the helpers, on the way to the dormitory, one of the bedroom doors burst open and we found ourselves confronted by Miss Simmons, Mrs. Nichols and about ten of the girls. Miss Simmons burst into song and all the other girls joined in. They strode all down the first flight of stairs and on to the landing singing lustily:

> *'Show me the way to go home,*
> *I'm tired and I want to go to bed.*
> *I had a little drink about an hour ago,*
> *And it's gone right to my head.*
> *No matter where I roam,*
> *On land or sea or foam,*
> *You will always find me singing this song,*
> *Show me the way to go home.'*

It sounded so funny to hear them singing this type of song, in a convent of all places, that Sheila and I started to laugh and laugh until the tears rolled down our faces. We laughed so much that I lost my balance and fell over, pulling Sheila on top of me, and as we lay on the stairs convulsed by giggles, we could see the 'choir', with their faces turned towards us, grinning from ear to ear. Suddenly I looked along the corridor and saw that the door to each small bedroom was open and from each doorway a face peered, wearing a look of absolute disgust. Seconds later the singers saw them, too, and walked down the stairs still singing, and Sheila and I picked ourselves up and went quickly to our bedroom. The next morning Sister Gabriel met us on the way to breakfast.

'I hear you have been enjoying yourselves,' she said brightly. 'I am so glad. I have had some complaints from the other guests about the noise you were making, but please do not take any notice of them.'

The whole time we were in France I felt as though I had a bad cold. My nose ran continuously and this affected my speech so much that people often could not understand what I was trying to say. Mrs. Nichols noticed the trouble and promised that when we returned to England she would ask her son-in-law, an ear, nose and throat specialist, to see me.

At last our holiday in France was over and we were left with only our souvenirs and a host of happy memories. I remembered again the lovely river trip we had enjoyed one day as the guests of the French Government, and the unforgettable sight of St. Michael's Mount rising as it were straight out from the sea. It all seemed rather like a wonderful dream as we sat once again in the car on our way to the night ferry and England.

We reached the dock gates and took our place at the end of a long queue of cars and coaches, but a friendly gendarme waved us on to the quayside and as we passed the other cars we received some rather inquiring glances from the occupants. A strong wind was blowing as we boarded the ship and I was glad to get into the lounge and sit in an armchair in the corner. Watching the porters carrying our luggage, a sudden thought struck me. 'I wonder if they have been through the Customs?'

Later I learned that the Customs officers had said they did not want to see the suitcases; they obviously thought we were too poor or honest to bring anything contraband through, and several of the girls humorously bewailed the fact that they had missed a golden opportunity.

Later that evening I went to the ship's side and watched the sun go down. Quite a number of the passengers kept coming and going and I stood there for a long time watching the sun disappear into the sea. It had been a wonderful holiday, and as God pulled the black curtain of night over the sky I could not help wondering what the future would bring. I was still standing there when Sheila came up and said, 'It's getting late. You had better have a nightcap and get to bed. The steward just told me that it might be rough tonight.'

Soon I was in bed and fell into a peaceful sleep only to be awakened by one of my cabin-mates being violently sick. Apparently she had been sick several times, and my eyes almost popped out of my head when the steward came in to empty the bowl. Fancy a strange man walking into our bedroom! It had not struck me that there were no stewardesses on the boat, and the few female attendants there had more than enough to do since over half the passengers seemed to be sick. I felt sorry for the poor girl who was being sick but knew I could do nothing to help her, and in any case she was being well cared for, so giving way to the overwhelming tiredness which possessed me I closed my eyes and slept soundly through the stormy night.

Next morning we were given breakfast as guests of the captain and then, as we said, 'Thank you and farewell,' to the members of the crew who had looked after us so well, I knew that the holiday was over.

15

New Horizons

Back at home life went on as before but I found there was very little I could do because of the pain in my nose. Eventually the specialist examined me and suggested that I should wear glasses. My nose was X-rayed, but I was never told what was really wrong with it apart from the fact that I have a buckled septum, and the specialist recommended an operation to remove a small piece of bone.

He explained that he could not perform the operation himself because I did not live in the area covered by his hospital, so an appointment was made for me to be examined by the ear, nose and throat specialist at one of the great London teaching hospitals. In the meantime my spectacles arrived, and with these I was able to read once again, but I could not concentrate for long without the pain returning.

After a thorough examination and X-ray in the London hospital the specialist asked, 'Have you ever been in hospital?'

'Oh, yes, more than half of my life,' I replied quickly. Then in answer to his further questions I told him a little of life in Queen Mary's.

He listened patiently and with obvious interest and then concluded the conversation by saying earnestly, 'I know Mrs. Collis and have seen her at work. She is a remarkable woman.'

A fortnight passed during which time I could hardly stop crying. I knew it was upsetting for other people to see me in this state, but somehow I could not help myself. The pain never eased by night or day, in fact it was worse when lying down, in spite of the fact that there were six pillows on the bed; so most nights it was impossible to sleep.

Eventually the day came for me to go to the hospital again to hear the result of the X-ray. A nurse helped me in to see the specialist while Mum remained outside. Mum thought it better that I should speak up for myself and besides this, although normally nothing makes her turn a hair, she just could not bear to see a nose examination in progress.

The specialist at the London hospital confirmed what the previous one had said, that my nose was buckled and an operation was the only way to put the trouble right. He asked whether I would like him to go ahead with the operation and for a moment I was silent. I wished desperately that Mrs. Collis could have been there, she would have known what was best. It was not that I was afraid of the operation, in fact it was not really a very serious one, but I knew it would upset my handicap and make it worse for quite a time. On the other hand I could not go on as I was, and the specialists had both said that there was no other way of overcoming the pain. My tongue was dry and seemed to cling to the roof of my mouth as I announced my decision, 'Do whatever you think is best. I do not mind.'

'All right, Vera. We will let you know as soon as we have a bed. You should not be in hospital for more than three or four days.'

It was November when a letter arrived from the hospital asking me to go to their extension at Orpington on the following day. I was so pleased to think that something was going to be done at last that I wept once again, but this time for joy. It was Thursday when Mum and Gladys took me by train to the hospital, and as they left I called, 'Don't worry, I shall probably be home by Tuesday.'

A young nurse undressed me and put me to bed and I leaned back against the pile of pillows trying not to think of the morrow. It was strange to be in a ward full of normal women, most of whom were in hospital for a minor operation only and would be going home in a few days' time. It was so different from the hospital for the 'chronic sick'. Here everyone was cheerful and seemed to treat the enforced stay in bed rather as a few days' well-earned rest from household chores and worries. In the afternoon the doctor came around, and after examining me he said warmly, 'If there is anything you want do not be afraid to ask. You can have anything you like, and all these pretty young nurses are here to wait on people like you.'

Later that night, when everyone was tucked down, I offered a silent prayer to God to help me through this difficult time.

After the usual preparation for an operation I do not remember much of the next morning. It was about 9.30 a.m. when I was given the anaesthetic, and I was surprised to find it was evening when I regained consciousness. I seemed to be in a sea of blood and two nurses were trying to sit me up. One thought passed through my mind, 'I am glad that Gladys is not here. She would have fainted at the sight of so much blood. I must help the nurses to sit me up or they might strain themselves.' Then I fell back into a deep sleep.

As the days went by the bleeding stopped, the plugs were removed, and I became stronger, but breathing was still painful. I found I was not breathing in the way I had been taught so many years before, so every day I put my hands on my chest and made myself breathe deeply and rhythmically until the correct method became once more a habit.

The operation had gone according to plan but as I had lost so much blood the doctors wanted to keep an eye on me for a little while longer, and it was ten days before they said I could go home. I still felt a little weak and expected to find that my handicap was much worse, but to my surprise, and to the delight of Mum and Gladys, I could do anything almost as well as a normal person. My hands did not shake and I walked without the fear of falling, but my joy at this discovery was clouded by a worry which no one else knew about—I found it impossible to do mental arithmetic or to remember anything, my brain seemed to be numb and just would not work properly. It was soon apparent what was happening; the drugs were still having an effect on my nervous system and as in time these effects wore off I began to get more and more shaky. It was not long before my movements became almost as uncontrollable as they had been ten years before and I began to worry lest I should never get better.

After months of hard work I began to make some headway, but this experience had shaken my confidence. Was I really the person to help cerebral-palsied people when apparently I didn't know enough about the way to help myself? Had all those dreams been girlish fancy? Was I trying to keep something alive that had died years before? I asked myself these questions over and over again. Did I really want to help people like myself or was it just that I was grateful to Mrs. Collis and had expressed these opinions to please her? However, if I gave up the idea of helping cerebral-palsied people, what else was there to do? There seemed to be no answer to these questions and the many more that chased each other through my head. I could paint a little and do knitting and needlework, but not well enough to earn a living by any of these means. Once again I turned to God for advice and patiently waited for His answer which came about six months later.

Jane, one of the staff of the unit, wrote to me one day to say that the doctor who had been the medical superintendent of Queen Mary's for many years had left there and had opened a home for cerebral-palsied adolescents, and she invited me to join her on a visit there. She came by car the night before and took me to her London flat where we had supper. I was quite amused to see the cup she gave me to drink from, it was an ordinary tea-cup with a small handle and I could not possibly pick it up without spilling the contents. On being reminded of this fact she offered me the only cup with a large handle she possessed—a beer mug!

We planned our route for the next day and then went to bed. The room I slept in was the largest bedroom I had ever seen and as Jane switched on the bedside lamp and bade me 'Good night', I felt rather like an ant on that wide expanse of floor and walked slowly to my nest in the corner. The following morning, after breakfast, Jane had a little shopping to do to buy the things needed for the picnic lunch we had planned, and while she was out I went back to the bedroom to get dressed. A little later the daily maid—a real Mrs. Mopp—arrived and called in to see how I was getting on. Several times she popped her head round the door and each time she murmured, 'Tut, tut. What a shame! The poor little thing!'

When she had come in for about the sixth time I shouted, 'I am quite all right, you know. I haven't jumped out of a window yet!' I laughed, but she obviously wasn't amused, and giving me a strange look she walked out and stayed out.

When Jane returned we started on our journey, and after about an hour on the road we reached 'Ponds' where we were given a warm welcome by the doctor. We had our picnic lunch indoors, and once during the meal the doctor came in to see if we had finished. He gave us an inquiring glance and then quickly said, 'I will come back presently.'

Jane and I looked at each other for an explanation and then both laughed as we realized that at the moment he had entered I had been drinking tea from the beer mug—perhaps he wondered why we had not asked him to join us in a quick one!

After lunch the doctor, Jane and I sat together in his large and comfortable sitting-room talking about all manner of things. Jane and I asked all the questions and the doctor did his best to supply the answers.

He told us that 'Ponds' had been opened a short time previously for young men and women who were badly handicapped with cerebral palsy and who were in the position in which I had found myself on leaving the unit—with the bleak prospect of spending the rest of their lives in a home for the chronic sick. At that time he did not have a definite plan for the future of 'Ponds', he did not know how or for what the children (as he called the ten residents) could best be trained, but in the meantime they all helped with the housework and were encouraged to cultivate a hobby.

As we sat there talking I suddenly realized that there were three people in the room and we all seemed to have something of interest to say to each other. So often I have been in a room where normal people are talking and when I have attempted to join in the conversation have been met with a glare or ignored; but here both Jane and the doctor listened to every word I said and gave straight answers to all my questions. They made me feel my proper age instead of a child amongst adults and I thought how much easier and pleasanter life would be if everyone had the intelligence to treat handicapped people in this way.

During our visit we were shown over 'Ponds' and were delighted with the way in which this lovely old mansion was being converted to take wheel-chairs and people who had difficulty in walking. Slopes were being built everywhere in place of steps and a new wing was being added to the back of the building overlooking the smooth green lawns.

Shortly before we left to return to London Jane slipped away to chat to one of the house mothers and I joined the young people in one of the large rooms with its magnificent views over the surrounding country-side. As they sat there, some in wheel-chairs, some in armchairs, listening to the radio and trying to keep their badly behaved bodies still, I realized that this was the sort of place I would like to work in. I wanted to help these people to learn to dress, wash and feed themselves, and to help them to help themselves. They were all very badly handicapped and it seemed an impossible task to teach them to be independent in any way, but on the other hand, remember how helpless I had been! So was it such an impossibility? Sitting there I wondered how I could ever have thought of giving up the idea of helping people with cerebral palsy when there was so much to be done. Some of these people were trying to weave scarves and make rugs, and some of them could type a little, so how much more could they do if they were trained properly?

All too soon Jane and I were on our way back to London, where a pleasant surprise awaited me. Jane had booked tickets for the ballet at the Royal Opera House, Covent Garden, and there we were joined by the parents of one of the ballerinas, who, after the performance, invited us to supper at a little French restaurant in the West End. I felt very grand and proud as the waiter asked what wine madam would like. I was being treated as a lady and I did my best to behave as one and to make my awkward body behave gracefully for once. The hands of the clock were creeping towards midnight as we reached Jane's flat once again; it was the end of a perfect day.

At home next morning it became crystal clear to me that before I could help anyone else I would have to convince people that I knew what I was talking about and the best way to do this would be to continue once again writing my autobiography.

At first I spent hours each day sitting at the typewriter in the bedroom, so that I would not be disturbed, but the machine was rather heavy and awkward to move, so when the summer came and Mum insisted I should sit in the garden to get more fresh air, the typewriter remained upstairs and I had to continue writing by hand. Soon I found my writing improved and before long it became quicker to write than to type. Spelling and grammar were still very bad and Jane and Gladys helped me with this by correcting my draft and typing it as it should be. Even though I could now write more quickly it was still taking too long, so one evening Gladys made a suggestion.

'Why don't you learn a little shorthand, Vera? It will be much quicker for you. I will write down a list of outlines for all the most common words, and then you can memorize them.'

'But you will never be able to read it,' I protested.

'I don't see why not. It will probably be easier than deciphering your atrocious spelling,' she said, with a laugh.

I found that shorthand writing with a ball-point pen was much simpler than it looked; a lot of the monotony was taken out of writing and now that I could get my thoughts on to paper more quickly it became easier to construct good sentences.

New Horizons

I continued writing, month in, month out, in sunny weather in the garden, in cold weather by the sitting-room fire, and whenever I came to a part that was rather difficult I visited Mrs. Collis at the unit where she was always ready to give her assistance.

A visit to a hospital is not everyone's idea of an enjoyable day out, but I looked forward to these days as something rather special. Quite apart from gaining physical and psychological guidance from Mrs. Collis it was always a thrill to see the children again and to be given such a warm welcome by children and staff alike.

Often before going into the schoolroom I have paused outside the glass door and have been amazed to see how normal the children look as they sit at their brightly coloured desks, working at their lessons, and it is sometimes difficult at first glance to understand why they are there at all and not in an ordinary school. They wear no special boots or leg-irons because they have no deformities to overcome, and their bodies are strong and healthy.

On a number of occasions my trips to the unit were arranged to coincide with a lecture or the showing of a special film to students and parents. One such film began by showing a married woman who had been born without arms, doing her housework and caring for her husband and family of several children, even to the point of changing the baby's nappy. Everything was done very efficiently with her feet and mouth, and the point of the film was to show that no matter how handicapped a person may be, so long as he has mental determination and is properly helped he can still lead a useful and happy life.

The film continued by showing the difference between normal, cerebral-palsied and simply mentally deficient children at various stages of babyhood and ended by giving some pictures of children at the unit and children of the same age group at a nursery school. With some of the children it was difficult to tell the difference between them, and as we sat watching my mind went back to the time before I knew Mrs. Collis when the very young children came into hospital, just as they were doing now, and wasted years of their lives by receiving the wrong or ineffective treatment. Then I thought of when I first knew Mrs. Collis and of all her difficulties before her work was recognized, and I realized just how far her work had progressed. She was still the same woman with the same ideas, but whereas once most people thought those ideas odd, or rather silly, they now came flocking to her for more and more of them. Many medical students came to the unit to be taught about development before going out to all parts of the world to carry on their work. As the film ended I brushed a tear from my eye; it was not a tear of sorrow but one of joy and pride, and all the way home in the hospital car my heart was still singing.

16

The End and the Beginning

CRISION

It is now summer 1956 and in a few weeks' time Gladys is to be married. It took me a very long time to get used to the idea of her courting and eventually marrying, as she had always seemed to have so little interest in the opposite sex. To be quite honest I was jealous of Ron, my future brother-in-law, when he and Gladys first met, because I knew it was extremely unlikely that I would ever marry and I felt resentful that anyone should occupy a higher place in her affections than me. However, in a short time Ron and I became friends and now I look upon him as my brother. Although Mum, Gladys and I have always been a self-sufficient little group since Dad and Stanley died, I have realized that it is often a blessing to have a man around the house, not only to tackle those jobs which are rather difficult for women, but also to give a more balanced outlook on life than can be attained in all feminine company.

Ron, who is a builder, is always ready to lend me a helping hand and has promised that he and Gladys will set up home with Mum and me, so the fear that at some time in the future I might be unwanted has been quashed. I know I shall always have a home, a home where I am welcome and which the family does not want me to leave, but apart from doing a little house-work, needlework, etc., how shall I fill the time?

There is an alternative. The doctor at 'Ponds' has offered me a place there and I am sorely tempted to accept, but if I go there I want it to be as a worker and not as a patient. I know there is a great deal I must be taught before I can teach and I am still hopeful that one day I shall be accepted for a course at a training college where I might possibly learn to improve my spelling and to do the complicated kind of arithmetic necessary for completing an income-tax return—just in case I ever earn enough money to need to complete such a form!

Often I remember with a smile how many sleepless nights could have been avoided and how overjoyed I would have been to have had such a place as 'Ponds' to go to when I was twenty-one. Oh, how times have changed, for now I can afford to be independent about the offer and choose whether or not I will accept.

Whatever happens in the future I know that God will help and guide me as He has always done along the many unusual paths which He has set before me. I always believe that like every human being I was sent to this earth for a purpose—that purpose is not always clear in youth, although part of it may have been accomplished already.

Looking back over the years I realize just how much my physical condition has improved; to summarize, I may say:

Speech. Is far from perfect, but is understandable to most people.

Feeding. I still use a spoon, as this is so much quicker than a knife and fork, but apart from needing the meat to be cut up for me, there are no difficulties.

Drinking. I always use a half-full mug with a large handle, or else a drinking straw, and then can manage alone.

Walking. Indoors and in the garden I walk unaided, although I still often tumble, and for short distances out of doors I walk quite well by linking arms with one or sometimes two other people.

Handiwork. Apart from an occasional jerk, when nervous or excited, my hands do not shake. I can thread and use a very fine needle for sewing and my embroidery compares favourably with that of a normal person.

Writing. At long last I have progressed to writing as against printing, and my penmanship is small and fairly neat. It still takes about three hours to write a short letter, but this is due to a greater extent to my inability to spell correctly, than to the actual time taken in writing.

Appearance. Occasionally I forget myself and wear a rather doleful expression, but for the most part I now look normal when sitting still. It is true children often stare when they hear my deep voice or see that I wear boots, which are easier to wear than shoes for walking. But children stare more out of curiosity than pity, for they realize that something is wrong, but they cannot quite make up their minds as to what it is.

Achievement. At a recent Ranger test I laid and lit a fire with one match, and then helped to cook a meal in a frying-pan. A few years ago I could not hold anything so small as a match box, and I most certainly would never have been able to strike a match.

Some days I make progress and sometimes I slip back a little, it depends to a large extent upon my state of health and frame of mind. The progress made is usually in such small stages as to pass almost unnoticed and it is only when meeting someone I have not seen for a long time that they remark on the improvement, and I realize with gratitude that I have taken another step towards independence.

A few weeks ago I received a telegram from Mrs. Collis, asking me to go to the unit on the following day. I was rather puzzled and surprised by the request because the following day was a Wednesday—the day on which Mrs. Collis holds her advice clinic during which her time is fully occupied with advising parents. What could be the reason for such an urgent summons, I wondered, as I dressed the following morning. Oh well, I would soon find out.

The hospital car took me to the unit, but it was not the old unit I knew so well; it had moved to new quarters. A block with rooms similar to those the unit had occupied previously had been repainted and decorated most tastefully in contemporary style, which gave it a delightfully modern appearance. The fixtures and fittings had been designed with a view to giving the children maximum independence; for instance, the toilets were very low, so that young children could sit on them unaided, and were fitted with press button flushes.

After a short tour of the new building, Jane grabbed my arm, 'Hi there, Vera, you should be down at the advice clinic. Mrs. Collis wants you to go down there straight away to meet someone.'

'Who is it?'

'You will find out when you get there!' The mystery deepened.

The advice clinic was temporarily being held in the Out-Patients' Department a few blocks away from the unit, and it came as quite a surprise when we walked in there to find that the department had been built in the first ward I had ever seen in Queen Mary's, the one to which I had been admitted so many years before. Jane saw that I was settled on a long bench next to some medical students and then left, as Mrs. Collis examined a child and explained to her audience what she was doing. It was a great pleasure to watch her at work as one child after another was brought in, and I felt greatly honoured to be given this privilege, but I could not help wondering who was this person I was to meet.

After a time Mrs. Collis said, 'The next child is ill and will not be coming; so we have a little time to talk, Vera. I asked you here today because I want you to meet someone from the B.B.C. He has read part of your book and he has also read *My Left Foot*, the book written by the cerebral-palsied Irish boy, Christie Brown. He would like to discuss a television programme about cerebral palsy, so I will introduce you and then you can get to know each other.'

She introduced me to a gentleman and lady who had been sitting at the other end of the room. This was the B.B.C. pro-

ducer and his assistant. I was so dumbfounded by all that was
happening that I sat in a kind of rosy haze listening as Mrs.
Collis told the producer about me. She said, 'Of course Vera
still has, and always will have, a very heavy disability, but she
has overcome it a great deal and I am sure she will go on improving because she is mentally normal and she knows what
she wants.'

It is true I do go on improving because I do know what I
want, but as Mrs. Collis told me on the way back to the unit
after the clinic had ended, 'One of your biggest handicaps,
Vera, is the fact that you are intelligent, and you still get frustrated because you cannot always do what you want to do. Life
gets very hard sometimes, doesn't it, but keep on trying, you
will be the conqueror in the end; and you know, Vera, you
might one day be on television as the star of the show! What
would you feel about that?'

Perhaps she was teasing me, but I looked ahead and the sky
suddenly seemed filled with a golden glow. I thanked God for
the greatest of all His blessings—Hope! But I remembered that
hope has to be backed by hard, intelligent work if dreams are
to be fulfilled, and I went home to finish this book.

Three Steps Forward

by VERA DEAN

Three Steps Forward is the exceptionally interesting story of an exceptional person. Vera Dean is handicapped in a way which has made life very hard for her; she is cerebral palsied. For the first fifteen years of her life she was unable to express her thoughts in speech or any other way that could be understood—nor could she do the simplest things for herself. In those days she, and others like her, were thought to be mentally defective and treated accordingly, and she was left without education. Yet within the prison of her disordered movement was a perfect intelligence and an independent spirit. She was aware of her predicament as she was taken from one hospital to another, and struggled to make herself understood. It was at this time that Mrs. Collis was starting the work that has done so much for the cerebral palsied. Her understanding of their problems and her new approach to these problems gave Vera Dean, and many others, hope where there had been none. For Vera Dean it was the beginning of a new way of life in learning to live to the fullest possible extent in spite of her handicap. She learned a competence which had previously been denied her. She began to make a life of her own and finally she wrote and typed out the story of her achievement.

These are the bare bones of a moving success story which yet has its dark moments. But through adversity Vera Dean made many friends. John, amongst others, will not be forgotten and those she knew then are still her friends. To an imaginative reader this book will bring a whole new field of experience, for it tells how an imprisoned spirit, in this world but isolated from it, broke through the barrier and joined us.